AND
FINALLY...

RYAN HERMAN

AND FINALLY...

THE WEIRD
AND WONDERFUL
WORLD OF NEWS

PAVILION

Pavilion
An imprint of HarperCollins*Publishers* Ltd
1 London Bridge Street
London SE1 9GF

www.harpercollins.co.uk

HarperCollinsPublishers
Macken House
39/40 Mayor Street Upper
Dublin 1
D01 C9W8
Ireland

10 9 8 7 6 5 4 3 2 1

First published in Great Britain by Pavilion
An imprint of HarperCollins*Publishers* 2024

ISBN 978-0-00-864800-8

This book contains FSC™ certified paper and other controlled sources to
ensure responsible forest management.

For more information visit: www.harpercollins.co.uk/green

Publishing Director: Laura Russell
Commissioning Editors: Frank Hopkinson and Lucy Smith
Editorial Assistant: Shamar Gunning
Design Manager: Alice Kennedy-Owen
Designer: Hannah Naughton
Junior Designer: Lily Wilson
Production Controller: Louis Harvey

Printed and bound in the UK using 100% renewable electricity at CPI Group
(UK) Ltd

CONTENTS

FOREWORD

———

Ian Jones is the editor of *Jeremy Vine*, a topical debate show on UK TV. He was previously the senior programme editor on *Channel 5 News* and started his career as a newspaper journalist. He explains why inspiring, improbable or bizarre stories at the end of the news can often matter as much as the headlines...

They say first impressions are everything – but so are the last. For me, the two most important stories when putting together a TV news programme are your lead story and the last story. You need a lead that has an immediate impact to hook people in and a memorable end item to close out the show. That final story can be something that will get people laughing and smiling or just make them feel a bit better about the day.

The nature of headline news means it is serious, often sad, infuriating and depressing. That's why the end item is so important.

A great 'And finally...' connects with emotions. It's more interesting – and more challenging – to find something different. An uplifting human interest story, an idiosyncratic slice of life, or sometimes just a bit of plain and simple fun.

There are occasions when something seems like a natural fit for an 'And finally...', such as a huge lottery win.

Then you have the press conference and an even better tale emerges behind the family that suddenly received all this money. Instantly, it becomes the main event of the day.

One such example appears in this book – the couple who won £115 million on the EuroMillions and then revealed what they were going to do with all that cash. And you know viewers will be thinking to themselves, 'How would I spend it?'

They are stories that also require a deft touch when it comes to writing, real empathy with the subject, and a rare gift that only some people have – comic timing. And it doesn't have to be slapstick. That's too obvious. A subtle or even dry sense of humour can really make the difference.

The best 'And finally...' reporters can make simple stories shine. They can cheer you up with a turn of phrase or some hilarious vox pop. They have that understanding that the reporter or the writer is the storyteller, and the subject is the star.

INTRODUCTION

———

In May 1993, Sir Martyn Lewis CBE gave a series of talks at universities across America about the state of TV journalism.

At the time, he was a newsreader for the BBC but had become jaded by the constant torrent of bad news that he was delivering nightly to the nation. He bemoaned the fact that his editors and producers often downgraded or simply ignored positive stories.

They stuck to the mantra of 'If it bleeds, it leads', an expression popularized at the beginning of the twentieth century by media tycoon William Randolph Hearst – the Rupert Murdoch of his day.

Sir Martyn was derided and, in some cases, misinterpreted. To put this in a modern context, when you go on to social media and people respond to a headline without reading the full story, to a degree that is what happened here.

He said that clearly tragedies, disasters and emergencies would always dominate the news agenda, and that focusing purely on good news 'would not be believable as an accurate picture of the world'.

But he also highlighted the example of ABC News in the USA, which was receiving mailbags of letters from people saying that the news made them feel hopeless. Subsequently, the broadcaster made a point of producing stories about people looking for 'legitimate solutions to seemingly intractable problems'.

It turned out that Sir Martyn was ahead of his time about the effect of being bombarded with bad news. There have been many studies into the 'negativity bias' of social media algorithms, designed to whip up confrontation, hatred and anger. There are now magazines, websites and feeds that are a pushback against that negativity.

As a newsreader, Sir Martyn presented hundreds of 'And finally...' stories and put his name to a book on the subject in 1984. He later said that those stories have their place, but the book you're reading now is closer to the agenda that he promoted in those speeches.

Here we have exactly the sort of daft 'And finally...' yarns one would typically expect, but also stories you won't expect or have ever heard of, as well as tales of people finding amazing solutions to problems.

This will be the only publication where you'll not only read about Charlie Blair, a woman who took hip-hop into care homes, but you'll also find out how a goat ended up becoming a punk rock icon. Plus, we feature Vasili Arkhipov, and if you don't know who he was, then once you read about what he did on a Soviet submarine in 1962, you'll be grateful that he existed.

Behind any story, there is usually another story. In the case of Sue Papadoulis, founder of the Good News Movement, you'll read about how a tragedy made her re-evaluate her career and set her on a path to promoting reports of positive events around the world.

There are people who made the headlines in the unlikeliest of circumstances, from a bunch of students being passed off as Leeds United, to the young officer who stole a tank from his army base and took it to his parents house, and the child refugee who changed her name from Stephanie to Steve to get businesses to buy her software products and then made 70 of her employees millionaires.

There is also Dan Davies' incredible account of the link between him, his wife and a mission that helped to crack the Enigma code.

And then there's Professor Andrew Deaner, whose story has a personal connection. A few weeks after he helped to save the life of footballer Fabrice Muamba I was lying on the same operating table casually chatting about football while he was threading a tube through one of my arteries to put in a stent.

Ultimately, this is a book about people (plus a few animals); people doing extraordinary, wonderful, ingenious, life-changing and, sometimes, utterly stupid things.

There is a quote that perhaps best sums it up, which can be found in the chapter about kindness, from filmmaker and author Ali Catterall. He says, 'I think we need stories that shake us out of our complacency. You know, things are magical, things are bizarre, things are peculiar because life is. You can find magic in a dustbin. It depends where and how you look.'

CHAPTER ONE

IT'S A

FAMILY

AFFAIR

THE ADVENTUREMEN

When he was only 12 years old, Shabir Haidary fled from his village in war-torn Afghanistan. It took him the best part of a year to reach the UK, through a combination of planes, boats, and walking on foot. He successfully applied for asylum and was placed with the McDonalds, a foster family in Gloucester.

Shabir was keen to get involved in combat sports. His foster mother, Ann McDonald, encouraged him to join the Fight Factory, a boxing club in Bristol. That was in 2014. Within three years Shabir had won a national amateur title and he has since turned professional.

Ann is also the mother to another inspirational character. Jamie McDonald is known as Adventureman. He has cycled from Bangkok to Gloucester since already introduced above, and has run 5,000 kilometres across Canada, which is all the more extraordinary when you learn that Jamie was born with a rare spinal condition that required frequent visits to the hospital throughout his childhood. Whenever he takes on a new challenge, he wears his Adventureman outfit, which was designed by Connor Reddy, who was ten years old at the time and has dyspraxia.

Meanwhile, having arrived in the UK without speaking a word of English, Shabir now has a degree in Sports Strength and Conditioning from the University of Gloucester and obtained his licence as a boxing coach in June 2023. As his own coach, Jon Pitman, says, 'He has taught me more than I've taught him. It makes you think about your life and kids. You moan about certain things but then you realize your problems are pretty minimal.'

MY STORY

Dan Davies

Dan is an award-winning author from the UK. Here he recalls the tale of an extraordinary connection that links him and his wife to a mission during the Second World War that helped to change the course of history...

❝ I was fast giving up on finding 'the one', specializing instead in relationships that ended in spectacular, if predictable, flameouts. My parents and siblings were losing hope of me ever settling down, too. But I hadn't quite relinquished hope, and sure enough, Iona was there, sitting quietly in the corner of the fashion cupboard at *Esquire* magazine when I first walked through the corridor into the editorial offices. I said hello and she looked up and smiled. My life changed in that moment, although I didn't know it at the time.

We first met in 2006. Two years later we were having dinner as a couple, and the subject moved to our families. I recounted how my grandfather, Gordon Connell, had been inspired to write his first book by what he described as 'an accidental encounter' with a war memorial in the Scottish Borders.

During a family caravan holiday in 1973, Gordon wandered off alone looking for somewhere to cash a cheque and perhaps find a drink. Under his arm he carried a battered pair of Zeiss binoculars with a swastika engraved on them. He was a Second World War veteran and the binoculars were a trophy taken from a German U-boat before it sank, taking with it his two comrades.

Looking up at the memorial, he came to an extraordinary realization; 'I find it difficult to describe my emotions,' he later wrote. 'The Lieutenant Anthony Blair Fasson, George Cross, Royal Navy, whose name appeared with many others, was the same Tony who had saved my life over 30 years before.' Connell's book, *Fighting Destroyer*, was published in 1976.

Back in 1942, advances in the German navy's Enigma code meant it had been almost ten months since the Allied Forces had last successfully deciphered U-boat signals. The blackout had led to heavy Allied losses. Then *U-559*, a German U-boat, was spotted off the coast of Egypt. Four British destroyers were despatched, including HMS *Petard*, to try to capture it. Gordon and Anthony were part of the crew on *Petard* and Gordon was given the order to lead a party onto the sub. The gap was too wide for him to leap onto the U-boat, so he was ordered to dive in from the upper deck and swim.

After a moment of hesitation, Anthony stepped forward and dived into the water along with Able Seaman Colin Grazier. The U-boat was beginning to fill up with water. As Anthony and Colin smashed open cabinets and grabbed documents, they passed them to 16-year-old Tommy Brown, the youngest member of *Petard*, who had ignored orders by joining his crewmates in the water.

Gordon, meanwhile, was rowing as fast as he could. When he and others from the *Petard* reached the U-boat, they found Tommy hanging on for dear life, while clutching documents.

The U-boat was now sinking and Gordon told Tommy that Anthony and Colin needed to come up immediately, but they went down with *U-559* and never resurfaced. Tommy died heroically three years later while trying to save his sister from a house fire, and Gordon passed away in 1992 before it came to light that those documents had allowed the British to crack what became known as the Enigma code, helping to change the course of the Second World War.

Robert Harris, whose book *Enigma* was made into a Hollywood movie, says that without Anthony, Colin and Tommy, 'there might never have been a D-Day in June 1944'.

When I finished telling the story, which has long been a source of pride for my family, Iona had her hand over her mouth. I asked her what was wrong. And it was then that she explained that the story of 30 October 1942 is as famous in her family as it was in mine. First Lieutenant Anthony Fasson, she said, was her great-uncle, the beloved older brother of her grandmother, Sheena.

In 2011, our first child, Iris, was born. Not long afterwards, Sheena, who was in her nineties, sat in the front row of the small church in Edzell, Scotland, to see Iona and I get married. On that beautiful September afternoon, in a marquee outside the home Iona grew up in, we cut our wedding cake with Anthony Fasson's ceremonial sword. **"**

SAME LIVES, DIFFERENT PLACES

Shortly before the outbreak of the Second World War, a woman in the USA gave birth to twins and immediately put them up for adoption. The Springers stepped forward and offered to take both boys, only to be told – incorrectly – that one of them had died. They christened their son James. Meanwhile, the other twin was adopted by the Lewis family, who also christened their son James. When James Lewis sought to find out about his family tree, imagine his shock when he was told not only did he have a twin, but his brother, James Springer, was alive and well.

When the Jim Twins, as they became known, met up aged 39, they soon realized they had a lot more in common than just physical appearance (the obvious difference being their hairstyles). So many aspects of their lives had been a mirror image. They both worked for McDonald's, became deputy sheriffs, drove a light blue Chevrolet, had married and divorced a woman called Linda, then both married a Betty, had brothers named Larry, went to Pass-a-Grille beach in Florida on holiday, and smoked and drank the same brands of cigarette and beer.

THE LITTLE LADY OF THE LAKE

———

In 2018, parts of Sweden had been hit by a drought, and when eight-year-old Saga Vanecek, who was on holiday with her family in Jönköping County, started paddling in the shallower-than-usual waters of Lake Vidösten she felt something strange and bumpy underfoot.

Reaching into the water she picked out an ancient sword, conjuring up images of the Lady of Lake and the Arthurian legend of Excalibur, although her father had a different literary figure in mind.

'She lifted it high above her head, and shouted as if she was Pippi Longstocking, "Daddy! I found a sword!"', explained Saga's father Andy, who was nonplussed at first, and far more interested in getting back home to watch the World Cup final between France and Croatia.

Upon closer inspection, Andy realized the object was indeed a sword. So, he sent pictures to a local archaeologist who said she 'got goosebumps' when she saw the images, and initially thought the sword dated back to the Viking era or possibly even earlier. The sword was then handed over to experts who confirmed that it was around 1,500 years old.

If you're an eight-year-old and you've just found an ancient sword you would probably want to go tell everyone about it.

But archaeologists wanted to trawl the lake to see if there were any other objects. So, Saga had to stay silent for three months, although she did tell her best friend, who swore (or maybe pinky swore) to keep the secret and was true to her word, while

Andy admitted, 'I think maybe I found it harder to keep secret than she did.'

AND FINALLY...

When Mary Grams from Alberta, Canada, lost her wedding ring, she couldn't bear to tell her husband so she went out and bought a cheap imitation. Mary kept up the pretence for 13 years, during which time her husband passed away, and the only other person who knew was her son. In 2017, her daughter-in-law found the ring when digging up some vegetables in Mary's garden – it was in the middle of a carrot.

HIDDEN GOLD

In 1938, the Sulzbacher family fled from Nazi Germany, escaping the persecution of the Jewish people. They sought refuge in Hackney, London, UK, and brought them with the family treasure in the form of gold coins, which Martin Sulzbacher stored in a bank vault.

When war broke out a year later, Martin was considered to be an 'enemy alien refugee' by the British government. Together with his wife and four children, he was put on the SS *Arandora Star*, a ship that was bound for Canada but sank after being torpedoed.

Amazingly, the Sulzbachers survived after spending several hours at sea. Martin was then sent to Australia, while the rest of his family ended up on the Isle of Man.

Meanwhile, Martin's brother Fritz, and five other members of the family, had remained in Hackney. The Nazis were raiding bank vaults across Europe and, according to one report, Fritz had discovered that the Sulzbachers were on a Nazi hit list. So, they decided to put the gold in two jars and they buried them in their garden, but tragically they died during one of the many German bombing raids that took place across London during the war. It was only when Martin and his family eventually returned to the city that they discovered that the coins had been moved, but they had no idea where they had gone.

Seven years after the war had ended, workmen found one jar of coins on a building site and it was traced back to Martin. Then, in 2007, the second jar containing 80 double-eagle coins was found by local resident and artist Terry Castle, who was building a frog pond in the garden of a care home with a team of volunteers.

Because Martin had passed away in 1981, a court ruled that the jar and its contents were legally the property of his four children.

They, in turn, handed over one of the coins in its original wrapper to the Hackney Museum. The remaining coins fetched £98,280 at auction and Martin's son, Max, said some of the money would go towards giving his deceased family members proper gravestones.

Terry, however, never received anything for his find other than a lot of hassle and people assuming he was rich, although the incident did spark interest in his work as an artist. 'I'm a free man, freer than I'd be if I had the treasure,' he said in an interview with *Spitalfields Life*.

Dr Roger F. Bland was Curator in the Department of Coins and Medals at the British Museum at the time and he said, 'The case of the Hackney gold coins is one of the most unique and compelling stories that we have been involved with. There is an incredibly human element to this discovery that is absent from many archaeological finds.'

In 2017, what became known as the Hackney Hoard was listed by the Portable Antiquities Scheme as one of Treasure20, England's 20 most significant finds.

WHERE THERE'S A WILL ...

———

The Wendels were a famously reclusive and seriously wealthy family who lived in a mansion on the corner of Fifth Avenue and 39th Street, about a third of a mile [0.5 kilometres] from the Empire State Building in New York. There were six sisters and one brother, John, a tyrannical figure who forbade any of his siblings from getting married. Eventually, one of them, Rebecca, broke rank and tied the knot, albeit when she was 61.

They didn't use electricity, they dressed from another era, and their mansion became known as the House of Mystery, but the Wendels' portfolio of properties would be worth billions today. They were contrary characters who would happily leave a building empty for years if they didn't find the right tenant but would charge significantly reduced rents to tenants they liked, and kept one site vacant so that local children could play there.

When Ella Wendel died in 1931, the family tree ended, and most of her $100-million estate was dispersed among various charities, including the Society for the Prevention of Cruelty to Animals in New York, which received $3.5 million. This is also where the myth of Ella's poodle, Tobey, was born. It was reported in the UK that Tobey was given $15 million in Ella's will, making him comfortably the richest animal in the world.

This story was circulated and published in different countries, although the numbers often changed, and sometimes they were inflated. *Vice* magazine ran a story in 2013, claiming Tobey's inheritance had been passed on from one dog to another and stood at $80 million. What *was* actually inflated was the truth. Tobey never received a cent, although it is said that he effectively became the sole permanent tenant of the Wendel mansion.

Several servants and caretakers ensured that he was well looked after until he passed away in 1933.

AND FINALLY...

When wealthy couple Steven Klinsky and Maureen Sherry bought an apartment on New York's Fifth Avenue in 2003 they hired architect Eric Clough. 'Can we do something for our kids?' they asked. Eric is famed for turning ordinary spaces into something extraordinary, and he created loads of hidden surprises within the walls of the apartment. Better still, he did so without telling the owners. Among the many surprises they discovered was a poem written by Steven hidden behind 24 wooden panels, as well as a Japanese wood puzzle that held the key to unlocking a hidden compartment, while clues for solving a scavenger hunt were carved into radiator covers. 'I kept sneaking back into the apartment and hiding a few more clues,' said Eric.

'SORRY, HOW MANY CHILDREN?'

S ome years ago, Scotland's *Daily Record* newspaper ran a competition for a family to win a trip to Italy. The prize also included £50 spending money per family member (around £270 in today's money). When the paper informed Joseph and Bridget Kennedy that they had won first prize, the news came as a lovely surprise. But the Kennedys also had a surprise of their own for the *Daily Record* when they told the paper that it be would forking out spending money, plus flights and accommodation, for their 15 children.

OH BROTHER, WHERE ART THOU?

———

When Irene Adkins was ten months old, she was abandoned by her parents, along with their three other children. They were left in a caravan, were taken into care by the children's charity Barnardo's, and were then given to different families. That was in 1932. Irene's biological parents would go on to have three more children, including Terry Spriggs, who was born in 1937.

Terry, who lived in Northamptonshire, UK, knew he had a sister called Irene but attempts to find her had proved fruitless until his niece started compiling a family tree. She began to join the dots through a combination of the social media website Friends Reunited, and going through library archives, and discovered Irene through the Barnardo's archive.

In 2010, Terry turned up at Irene's house in the neighbouring county of Oxfordshire. 'I did not know if it was the right place, and I did not know what reception I would get when I got here, but life is too short,' Terry said.

They continued to meet up weekly until her 80th birthday, when Irene assumed she was going for a meal with a very small group of close family friends.

The *Oxford Mail* reported that the Spriggs family had brought together more than 50 relatives for a surprise party, many of whom Irene was meeting for the first time. Terry's daughter, Mandie, said, 'I lost my mum when I was 18 months old, and it is like I am looking at my mum through her.'

WHAT'S IN A NAME?

———

When John and Margaret Nelson of Chesterfield, UK, sat down to think about what name they would give to their newborn baby daughter, they drew up a list of 279 possibilities. Then they whittled it down... to just 139.

When it came to putting those names on a birth certificate, the Nelsons were told by the registrar there would only be room for 20. Plus, one can imagine the headaches when it eventually came to filling in a form for a passport or getting a bank account.

But the Nelsons stood firm and, after she arrived in late 1985, John and Margaret's new bundle of joy would be named... Tracy Mariclaire Lisa Tammy Samantha Christine Alexandra Candy Bonnie Ursala Zoe Nichola Patricia Lynda Kate Jean Sandra Karren Julie Jane Elizabeth Felicity Gabriella Jackie Corina Constance Arabella Clara Honor Geraldine Fiona Erika Fillippa Anabel Elsie Amanda Cheryl Alanna Louisa Angie Beth Crystal Dawn Debbie Eileen Grace Susan Rebecca Valerie Kay Lena Margaret Anna Amy Carol Bella Avril Ava Audry Andrea Daphne Donna Cynthia Cassie Cristabel Vivien Wendy Moira Jennifer Abbie Adelaide Carrissa Carla Anne Astrid Barbara Charissa Catalina Bonny Dee Hazel Iris Anthea Clarinda Bernadette Cara Alison Carrie Angela Beryl Caroline Emma Dana Vanessa Zara Violet Lynn Maggie Pamela Rosemary Ruth Cathlene Alexandrina Annette Hilary Diana Angelina Carrinna Victoria Sara Mandy Annabella Beverly Bridget Cecilia Catherine Brenda Jessica Isobella Delilah Camila Candace Helen Connie Charmaine Dorothy Melinda Nancy Mariam Vicki Selina Miriam Norma Pauline Toni Penny Shari Zsa-Zsa Queenie Nelson.

When football fanatic Trevor George applied the 20-name rule following the birth of his daughter Jennifer, he put her full name down on the birth certificate as:

Jennifer Pele Jairzinho Rivelino Alberto Cesar Breitner Cruyff Greaves Charlton Best Moore Ball Keegan Banks Brooking Curtis Toshack Law George.

Presumably he left out Di Stefano as it would have taken up two names. To coin an old Australian expression, the birth certificate made Trevor as popular as a rattlesnake in a lucky dip with his wife, Lynette. She walked out, and it wasn't because he failed to include Puskas, Eusebio or Dalglish. They resolved their differences a month later and their daughter was renamed as Jennifer Anne George, which was far more practical, albeit far less entertaining.

YOU'RE NEVER TOO OLD FOR LOVE

R on Owen and Ruth Holt from the UK worked in the same office and briefly dated back in the 1950s. Ron was a bit of a Romeo and was engaged to another woman, Moira. So he broke things off with Ruth. He never married, and went on to become Ronnie Ray, a cruise ship entertainer, and later became a football scout for Fulham and Norwich City. Meanwhile, Ruth got married and moved to Saudi Arabia, had two sons, and got divorced in 1983.

Then, in 2014, they were reunited when Ruth was 75 and Ron was 80. Unbeknown to each other they had both moved into the same housing complex. Ruth asked the warden if it was the same Ron Owen. She knocked on his door. At first, he had no clue who she was, but then they got chatting and rolled back the years. Four years later they got married.

'I don't think I cared for anybody else like I cared for him,' said Ruth a few weeks before they tied the knot, while Ron said, 'I've never been this happy'. Awww.

IF AT FIRST YOU DON'T SUCCEED...

When American celebrity and socialite Tommy Manville died in 1969, he had been married 13 times, although it could have been more. Even Tommy himself may have lost count towards the end, given that that figure included two remarriages.

The press certainly struggled to keep track. A report dated 11 August 1952 revealed that 'Tommy Manville yesterday announced his divorce from wife number nine and his engagement to wife number ten'.

In actual fact, it was wife number nine. The tenth Mrs Manville came along five years later, when Tommy was 63 and he married 26-year-old Texan showgirl Pat Gaston.

When Ms Gaston's mother was asked about her son-in-law's previous nine marriages she remarked: 'I feel that he's been searching for something.'

As a young playboy, Tommy showed little interest in the family business (the Manvilles made their money from asbestos), putting one in mind of the line from Spinal Tap's keyboardist Viv Savage, who wanted to 'have a good time, all the time'.

In an attempt to get Tommy to settle down, his elders drafted a contract that guaranteed him $250,000 if he got married. Yet they left out one small but very significant detail, by failing to stipulate that Tommy should only receive that sum on his first marriage.

Instead, every time he found a new bride, Tommy got another $250,000 pay-out, which would have been worth millions in today's money. A report in the *New York Times* claimed that before each marriage he guaranteed each new wife $50,000, although he also shelled out around $3 million on divorce settlements.

Tommy's longest marriage lasted 11 years, while the shortest didn't even make it to the end of the day. He separated from his seventh wife after eight hours.

AND FINALLY...

The celebrity who holds the record for the most marriages is Zsa Zsa Gabor, with nine. Among her many quotable one-liners on love and marriage, she said, 'I want a man who's kind and understanding. Is that too much to ask of a millionaire?'

BROUGHT TO BOOK

It was described as 'the ultimate *Cash in the Attic* story', albeit without an actual attic. Gene Johnson and her son Tony were doing a house clearance in Pinner, north-west London, UK, after Gene's sister had passed away, when they found a Chinese vase resting on a slightly wobbly bookcase.

It turned out that the vase dated back to the 18th century. Quite how it landed in Pinner is a mystery, although the likeliest explanation is that it was stolen by British troops sometime around 1860, when Beijing's Summer Palace was looted during the Second Opium War.

Tony took the vase to Peter Bainbridge, an auctioneer based in west London. Peter reportedly thought it was worth around £100,000 but he vastly underestimated its value. It went to auction in 2010 and the asking price started at £1.9 million. A bidding war broke out and when Peter shouted 'sold', the figure stood at £43 million.

Then the problems started. An extra £8.6 million was due to go to Peter – the broker gets a commission for any auction house sale in the UK – but the buyer refused because he thought the commission fee was too high. There was even speculation at one point that this was one of several fake bids instigated by the Chinese government at auctions, to set about a legal claim for what they would argue was rightfully theirs.

Although Peter tried to negotiate with the buyer, he was not allowed to reduce his fee because that may have triggered a chain of events that could have ultimately resulted in the Johnsons losing legal ownership of the vase. The 'fake bid' story proved to be, well, fake. Even so, it took two years before the vase was auctioned again. This time it was sold for £25 million, still a phenomenal amount of money for a vase left on a wobbly bookcase.

HAVING THEIR CAKE AND EATING IT... AND EATING IT... AND EATING IT

———

There's an episode of *Seinfeld* where Elaine Benes devours a vintage cake from King Edward VIII's wedding that would have been 60 years old when the episode was broadcast. Just how long could a wedding cake remain edible?

In a tradition that dates back to 19th-century England, newlyweds would save the top tier of their wedding cake for the christening of their first child. That tradition has been adapted over the years, so now couples will freeze the top tier of that cake and then have a slice to celebrate their first anniversary. David and Anne Cowburn not only maintained the tradition but kept it going and going. They would slice off a small piece of cake not just for the first anniversary but every subsequent anniversary.

The couple got married in 1970 and only ate their final slice in 2019. According to a report in the *New York Post*, they had watched a game show called *I've Got a Secret*, in which panellists were tasked with trying to find what the contestants were trying to hide. One couple said, 'We're going to eat the last piece of our wedding cake tonight. It's twenty-five years old!'

The Cowburns baked the last remaining crumbs into a new cake to celebrate their golden wedding anniversary in 2020.

AND FINALLY...

Julio Mora and Waldramina Quinteros from Ecuador hold the record as the world's oldest married couple, clocking in at 215 years (Julio died aged 110, when Waldramina was 105). If their parents had had their way, the couple would never have tied the knot, because both families disapproved of the relationship. So, Julio and Waldramina got married in secret back in 1941 and remained together until October 2020 when Julio passed away, two months after they set that record.

CHAPTER TWO

THE

CHANGE

MAKERS

FIRST AMONG EQUALS

———

Dame Stephanie Shirley came to the UK in 1939 at the age of five, as part of the Kindertransport programme that helped thousands of children to flee Nazi-occupied territories across Europe. 'That traumatic start made me determined to make mine a life worth saving,' she says.

Her local girls' school in Oswestry, Shropshire, didn't teach maths, so she successfully sought permission to take lessons at the boys' school instead. In the 1950s Stephanie got a job at the Post Office Research Station in Dollis Hill, London, and learned how to write computer code, but despite her best efforts to progress in her career, she routinely came up against sexism.

'That is what triggered me, in 1962, to set up a software company of women, designed by women; the sort of company I would like to work in,' she recalls. 'It was revolutionary. There were many women experienced in computing who had left the industry, as was the norm back then, to get married or when their first child was expected. And they were keen to work.' However, there was another major hurdle to overcome.

'I was writing dozens of letters a week to prospective customers to arrange meetings and getting absolutely no response, not one.' Stephanie's husband made a suggestion: why not try using a man's name instead? So, Stephanie became Steve.

'Hey, presto! Doors opened and the work came in! As entrepreneurs we have to make our mark. When you start small, you have to be memorable.'

Stephanie also gave every employee a stake in the company, which became known as Xansa, and when the business was eventually sold in 2007, she became a millionaire, along with 70 of her colleagues.

'The final stage of my work life is as a venture philanthropist,' she adds. 'I've given away some £70 million by investing in social ventures, mainly in the two things I know and care about: information technology and autism, which was my late son's condition. I also believe philanthropy can introduce new concepts to a business, you come into contact with a lot of people you're unlikely to encounter otherwise.

'I think that people who are poor (or were poor, as I was) better understand poverty and its difficulties, so it's more automatic for them to give. When it comes to persuading better-off people to give, the most crucial thing – as I stressed when I was the UK's ambassador for philanthropy in 2009–10 – is to show that giving is not a duty; it's actually a sheer pleasure.'

AND FINALLY...

On 27 February 2024, Ruth Gottesman addressed the students at Albert Einstein College of Medicine in the Bronx, New York, USA. What they didn't expect was that Ruth would announce that she was donating $1 billion to the school to ensure those students and future generations would never have to pay for their tuition fees. That worked out to $200,000 for each student in fees wiped out. You can imagine the reaction. Ruth is an educator and wife of the wealthy financier David Gottesman. Before he passed away in 2022, he instructed Ruth to take his fortune and 'do whatever you think is right with it'.

FAKE IT 'TIL YOU MAKE IT

———

A round 21 million people of Asian origin live in America, but Jevh Maravilla and Christian Toledo rarely saw any Asian faces in McDonald's ad campaigns. In June 2018, they made a life-sized poster of Christian holding a burger, while Jevh held an empty carton of fries – the fries were subsequently photoshopped into the shot. They put a golden arches logo on it, with the tagline 'I'm Lovin' It'.

Jevh then purchased a replica McDonald's staff shirt for $7.99, gave himself the name Jeff Bergara, passed himself off as a McDonald's Regional Coordinator, and along with three friends, put up the poster inside a Houston branch of McDonald's.

Then, in September, Jevh posted on Twitter (or whatever it is called these days): 'I noticed there was a blank wall at McDonald's so I decided to make this fake poster of me and my friend. It's now been 51 days since I hung it up.'

The post got over 840,000 likes. Then McDonald's got in touch and presented Jevh and Christian with a cheque for $25,000 each, which would be their fee for appearing in an ad campaign that was released later that year.

Jevh also gave numerous interviews and talks to open a discussion about advertising and stereotypes.

———

AND FINALLY...

'On her tiptoes, with fists clenched, the Nike model celebrates her form: "My butt is big and round like the letter C... It's a space heater... It's my ambassador to those who walk behind me,'" wrote *The Atlantic* magazine in 2010 in response to a Nike ad with the slogan 'My Butt is Big'. It prompted numerous commentators to write about Nike's move towards a more body-positive approach. But the ad was fake – how they spelt ambassador (in this case, 'embassador') was one giveaway. But, also, Nike had done virtually the same ad five years earlier.

Typos in ads for big brands can slip through the net. In 2023 a massive billboard was meant to say MULTI TASTY MULTIGRAIN PRINGLES, but instead it read MULTI TASTY MULTIGRAN PRINGLES. You can put that down to an 'age-old' mistake. We're here all week, folks!

MY STORY

Sue Papadoulis

Sue is the founder of the Good News Movement – a website and campaign that promotes positive stories. She talks about why she turned her back on a career in broadcasting and how a passion project based in Australia is helping to spread good news around the world...

❝ I worked as a journalist in Australia and then the UK for ten years. By the time I returned home to Australia, I was the news editor at Talkback Radio. Our news was syndicated to a vast array of regional networks, plus three radio stations using the same stories. There would be literally hundreds of bulletins every half hour. That comes with a lot of responsibility, and it was around that time that I really started to think about the impact I was having, and it was largely negative. Somewhere along the line, my goal of changing the world or righting wrongs, the things that motivate many people to first become a journalist, got lost in my own ego.

One day, I got into work at 5 a.m., and the first thing you do in the newsroom is call the emergency services to find out if there are stories, and usually, you know it's going to be bad news.

There had been a terrible accident. My first thought was 'Good, I've got a story for the morning bulletin.' I didn't think about the people involved or the consequences of what had happened. The police said a child had been killed. Later that morning, they released the name of that child (to the media) because they'd told the immediate family. I read out the story and included the child's identity, without the family being warned in advance. I came out of the studio, and then one of my staff said there was a call for me. 'I think it's the mother of the kid who got killed.' She said it in such a blasé way, without a care in the world. Of course, the mother was devastated. I had no adequate response other than 'Sorry'.

I changed the news policy so we wouldn't release names. I also thought there should be more good news in our bulletins. I instructed my team to go out and find those stories. That took time because there's a mistrust of journalists. Then, after two days of running those stories, my boss told me to 'get it off the air' because 'nobody wants good news'.

So I walked away, because I wanted to use media as a force for good. After a spell in PR, I became a mother and started my own PR firm, Profile Media. I started employing ex-journalists who, like me, were done with being in that negative environment. Then about five years ago, we launched our passion project, the Good News Movement.

There are, of course, many bad things happening in the world, but there is a negativity bias within us, which news organizations feed into. There is a project that started in Denmark called Constructive Journalism; it is a different way of structuring a story to provide people with an opportunity to take action, to feel empowered, rather than disempowered by just thinking 'this is terrible', and there's nothing that anyone can do.

One of my favourite Good News Movement stories happened when one of our team was driving through the Blue

Mountains in New South Wales on holiday. There was a traffic jam, and she saw this traffic warden dancing as he was giving signals.

She posted a video; somebody recognized him and tagged him in the comments. We got in touch with him, discovered he was a performer who wasn't making a living, so he became a traffic warden but was still entertaining people. We sent it to a national breakfast TV show. They loved it, ran the story, got him into the studio to be interviewed, and his career took off. It's a great lesson of being in the moment, choosing happiness and spreading that happiness to other people.

But there are also a lot of serious stories that are good news but can get overlooked. World hunger is at its lowest level for twenty-five years; the giant panda is no longer on the extinction list, childhood cancer rates are falling...

We usually find that people really connect with those personal stories, someone who has been positively impacted or a random act of kindness. I also think corporations globally have a responsibility here. Well, why can't corporations be sharing positive content because everyone has a platform? I think if we start affecting change at that level, that's when we'll start to see a shift happening across society.

Our PR firm, Profile Media, now sees itself as a good news consultant for organizations, helping them share their positive impact on the planet.

I needed to right wrongs. I guess if I hadn't had those experiences and hadn't come face-to-face with the impact I had, I wouldn't be on the trajectory that I'm on now.

As long as you learn a lesson and you do something positive about it, then I think you're in a good place. "

THE BRINGERS OF GOOD NEWS

---

1. MICHELLE FIGUEROA AND THE (OTHER) GOOD NEWS MOVEMENT

Michelle Figueroa was a freelance writer and reporter who was constantly trying to pitch positive stories to magazines and news channels but couldn't get anyone to publish them. One day, she was off sick, stuck in bed, and then decided to take control of her situation rather than remain at the mercy of an editor. In 2018, she started an Instagram feed known as @goodnews_movement; at the time of writing, that movement has over 5 million followers.

Then in 2022, Michelle compiled a collection of stories about random acts of kindness by kids around the world called *A Good Thing Happened Today*. She visited schools across America to promote the book with her Kindness Tour. The book includes the story of a young Danish girl who was troubled that her neighbours were lonely. So, the girl would put on a postman's uniform and deliver them kind letters.

One of those stories that Michelle pitched but couldn't get any takers for was about her neighbour, Michael. He had been due to be sent to the Auschwitz concentration camp along with his mum, who made teddy bears for a living. 'The Nazis wanted the bears for Christmas, so she told them if she and her son were sent to Auschwitz, they wouldn't have cuddly toys for their kids for the holidays,' explained Michelle, who now takes Michael to a clinic for his regular eye tests – and he still has his childhood teddy bear.

2. POSITIVE NEWS

In the early 1980s, Shauna Crockett-Burrows moved to northern Scotland and became a member of the Findhorn Foundation, a unique community that built an eco-village that would become a model for sustainable living. It was there that Shauna started a local newsletter that eventually morphed into *Positive News,* a quarterly magazine.

Shauna passed away in 2012 and three years later, *Positive News* launched a 'crowdfunding cooperative' that would result in it being owned by 1,525 readers across 33 countries.

In their own words, 'All profits are reinvested in creating inspiring journalism for the public benefit. Our directors are elected by and from our community of co-owners.'

More than 30 years after publishing its first issue, *Positive News* is still going strong, and also produces a weekly newsletter that highlights 'What went right this week'.

3. EMILY COXHEAD AND *THE HAPPY NEWSPAPER*

Emily is a UK-based designer, illustrator and all-round maker of happy things who realized that spending too much time watching the news and reading about it on social media was having a negative effect.

In December 2015, the first copies of *The Happy Newspaper* were printed after 73 people had pledged a total of £1,379 to provide a platform for positive news and wonderful people.

The paper now has well over 20,000 subscribers across more than 30 countries, and for every two copies that are sold, a free copy gets sent to a school. 'I don't pretend that everything is covered in sunshine and rainbows, because it's obviously not,' she says, but the paper serves as a reminder that there is good news, even if sometimes you must go looking for it.

THE BUILDING THAT MAKES KIDS WANT TO GO TO SCHOOL

W hat would happen if you allowed kids to design their own school? The answer can be found at the Colegio Reggio, in Encinar de los Reyes, on the outskirts of Madrid, Spain. The school was designed by architect Andrés Jaque following hours of interviewing children and asking them how they wanted their school to look. 'I want it to feel like a garden. Or a spaceship,' said one. 'A school with no walls,' said another.

The entrance to Colegio Reggio resembles a drawbridge. The exterior is covered in a thick layer of cork, and some classrooms look out onto gardens, some of which can't be accessed by the pupils because they are home to different types of wildlife, including birds, butterflies and bees.

Andrés is famous for outlandish buildings, such as the House in Never Never Land in Ibiza, which was built on stilts. When asked to explain what gave him the idea to take on the project of designing a school, he said that architectural environments can spark a desire in children 'for exploration and inquiry'.

AND FINALLY...

The majority of goods that come onto the island of São Vicente in Cape Verde, off the coast of West Africa, are transported in barrels. When architects Eloisa Ramos and Moreno Castellano were tasked with creating the National Centre for Art, Crafts and Design (CNAD), they decided to cover the whole exterior with multicoloured barrel lids.

Those lids help to create a passive cooling ventilation system, plus every colour represents a note that forms part of a musical score composed by Cape Verdean musician Vasco Martins. 'The culture of recycling is an integral part of the life of these islands – people know how to treasure every resource and empty drums are never wasted,' said the architects.

MAKE HYGIENE POVERTY HISTORY

Millions of people live below the poverty line in the UK and in the more extreme cases, some have to make choices between food and hygiene. The everyday items that everyone else takes for granted, such as toothpaste, deodorants, shower gels and tampons, are out of reach.

In 2018, journalist, broadcaster and author Sali Hughes teamed up with beauty industry PR Jo Jones to make hygiene poverty history. They had exchanged stories about teachers they knew who had bought toiletries for their pupils, and inspired by those stories, the pair decided to found the charity Beauty Banks. As two people working in the beauty industry, they had the contacts and know-how to generate publicity for their campaign.

It took one Instagram post by Sali to spark interest from dozens of media sites and donations from big brands, with high street chain Superdrug partnering with the charity to set up drop-off bins in their stores around the UK.

As Sali explains on the charity's website, 'How we look, smell and feel matters to our mental health, physical wellbeing, employment prospects, our future opportunities and personal relationships with others. No one should ever have to choose between putting food on the table or soap on their face.'

When Nicholas Lowinger was five years old, his mother, an art therapist, took him to a homeless shelter in Rhode Island, USA. Nicholas was wearing a brand-new pair of trainers, while the kids at the shelter either had shoes that were falling apart, or they were barefoot. That moment stuck with him. Aged 12 he became the founder of Gotta Have Sole, which has collected and donated trainers for over 100,000 children living in homeless shelters.

ALL HEART

M ick Jackson is a Scottish entrepreneur who went through a near-death experience in 2001 on K2 in the Himalayas, the world's second highest mountain. On the ascent, Jackson's Kashmiri guide, Sher, suffered a collapsed lung brought on by the effects of extreme altitude. There had already been one fatality on the expedition and Mick spent the next four days carrying, sometimes dragging, Sher down the mountain to where the air was less thin. Mick eventually collapsed, only to be revived by a four-year-old girl who found him and gave him water.

Reflecting some years later on what happened, Mick told *The Scotsman*: 'It clarifies who you are and your deepest values. It cuts through all the transient nonsense in our culture. It cuts through to who you are.'

He thought about how he could find a way to give to those less fortunate and he had an epiphany, although the grand vision may surprise you; it was selling office supplies. He asked a friend how much her company spent on paper, toner, pens, paper clips and so on... The answer was £250,000. 'I can do that,' Mick insisted, without any idea how.

Mick soon figured it out and set up the WildHearts Group, which describes itself as a 'world leading social enterprise, providing office supplies and print to the world's biggest companies'. A percentage of the company's profits go into a programme that helps to educate young entrepreneurs built around the United Nations' Sustainable Development Goals. The group also operates mission-led microfinance institutions in Malawi, Zambia and Zimbabwe, providing training and business loans for women living in those countries. While microfinancing isn't a failsafe solution, so far that support has helped to lift over 70,000 women out of poverty.

KIND OF BLUE

———

In 1980 the Belgian artist Jean Verame painted some rocks in a part of the Sinai Desert blue, the colour of peace, to celebrate the 1979 Egyptian–Israeli peace treaty.

With the blessing of Egypt's president, Anwar Sadat, Verame spent six months painting the rocks in an area that had been a battleground in the 1967 war between Egypt and Israel, using 10 tonnes of paint donated by the United Nations.

The story goes that when the project was announced to the press, something got lost in translation. It was assumed that the reason Verame was spending all that time painting was because he was producing giant canvases of the desert. When the penny dropped that he was actually painting giant rocks and boulders blue, it drew a less than enthusiastic response from some politicians and conservationists.

Over time, though, the Blue Desert became not only a popular tourist attraction but also an enduring monument to peace.

AND FINALLY...

When, in 2011, the tallest tree in Wales was damaged following a storm, Natural Resources Wales, which was responsible for the site, decided to commission somebody to carve what was left of it. Simon O'Rourke is an artist whose tool of choice is a chainsaw. He created a magnificent 50-foot [15-metre] sculpture, known as the Giant Hand of Vyrnwy. 'I loved working on the hand sculpture, it reminded me just how small we are compared to some of the living organisms on this planet! All in all, a humbling experience!' said Simon.

THE BOOK LADY

O n her first day in a new job as an English teacher at Roselawn High School in Turlock, California, USA, the first thing Tricia Garcia did when she stepped on campus was to ask where the reading books were kept. 'I was absolutely shocked when I was told there simply weren't any,' says Tricia, who also teaches journalism at Roselawn High.

'How am I supposed to encourage a love of reading when there is nothing to read? I quickly turned my shock and dismay into drive and motivation. I made it my mission to bring a library to my campus and began looking for and applying for grants.'

That was back in 2021, and those initial grant applications were knocked back, which only hardened Tricia's resolve. 'My principal brought up in a meeting that we had some extra funds and he was looking for a good place to allocate them. I immediately suggested the purchase of books to start a library.

'As part of the grant application process I had to develop a comprehensive list of the books I would purchase. I consulted a librarian and a couple of websites to look for popular young adult books. It was important to me that this library be stocked with books that would interest and intrigue my students. I looked for modern novels written in a language that is understandable to those students (many of whom speak English as a second or third language).

'I made sure that my list covered a diverse range of authors, including LGBTQ+ authors and books about those characters, authors with disabilities and/or writing about disabilities and neurodivergence, authors of colour and stories about people of colour, female authors and stories about girls and women, stories written about and by immigrants, and so on. I also wanted to include a variety of types of novels, nonfiction and fiction, graphic novels, and poetry.'

Then, on 11 August 2023, Tricia posted a picture of that library on Twitter and wrote, 'Before I came to my tiny alternative high school two years ago there was not a single novel on campus. I made building a library my mission. This year, students have access to 300 novels, hand chosen by me. My heart is full.'

Looking back on that moment, Tricia says, 'Posting that picture on Twitter was my victory lap. I had to do extensive research for this, providing academic sources to back up the need for and effectiveness of a quality school library. I worked late and early, applying for every grant I could find, writing word after word, begging someone, anyone, to help me get the supplies I needed to begin fostering a culture of reading on my campus. I am grateful to my principal, Felipe Meraz, for his support and trust in me.'

Tricia has a degree in creative writing and harboured ambitions of becoming a novelist. 'As time passed, however, I learned two things: teaching is very time-consuming and demanding (leaving little time or energy for writing) and working with teenagers is a greater joy than crafting even the finest sentence. It was one of the best feelings in the world to see those books on those shelves until I saw books in the hands of my students. And then *that* was the best feeling in the world.'

AND FINALLY...

She is one of the queens of country music and a phenomenally successful businesswoman, but to a countless number of children Dolly Parton is better known as the Book Lady. In 1995 she established the Imagination Library, a programme that posts free books to children. Dolly got the inspiration from her father, who never learned how to read. 'Before he passed away, my Daddy told me the Imagination Library was probably the most important thing I had ever done. He was the smartest man I have ever known, but I know in my heart his inability to read probably kept him from fulfilling all of his dreams.'

BREAKING THE GLASS

———

The 'glass ceiling' is an expression used to describe the invisible barrier that has historically prevented women and minorities from being promoted. When American Marilyn Loden passed away in 2022, obituaries all led on the fact that she was the woman who first came up with that expression back in 1978. Marilyn was working in Human Resources for the New York Telephone Company (NYTC), when she was invited to join a panel to talk about female advancement. Her company's vice president couldn't make it, and Marilyn happened to be the final speaker.

Having listened to people trotting out lazy stereotypes on why women didn't get ahead at work, she stood up and argued that they often came up against an invisible glass ceiling. Three years later, Marilyn quit NYTC when told to take a job she didn't want. She became a successful speaker, lecturer, author and adviser to organizations including the US Navy, where she helped bring about significant changes, including a ban being lifted on female sailors serving on submarines.

SERVING DEMOCRACY

The date 3 February 2022 marked the reopening of a cultural landmark in Downtown Los Angeles, USA.

Clifton's Cafeteria has a live redwood tree as the centrepiece of its main dining room. A stream runs through the cafeteria, which is also home to all sorts of curios, including a 250-pound [113-kilogram] meteorite and real dinosaur eggs.

However, it is the man who founded Clifton's that makes this place truly special.

Clifford Clinton's parents were both members of the Salvation Army and Clifford devoted much of his life to helping those most in need.

Clifford opened his first cafeteria in LA in 1931, during the Great Depression and, at its peak, there were eight Clifton's across America.

It became known as 'The Cafeteria with the Golden Rule', which allowed diners to choose how much they could pay. Every bill that a customer received for their meal was printed with the following words: 'Regardless of the amount of this check, our cashier will cheerfully accept whatever you wish to pay – or you may dine free.'

Clifford was also a leading figure in a campaign to rid Los Angeles of corruption, which was rife throughout the city. He received death threats and his restaurants suddenly started receiving random health and safety visits from city officials determined to make life difficult for him.

That campaign successfully ousted both the Mayor of Los Angeles and the city's Chief of Police in 1938.

Clifton's also welcomed guests of all races and creeds, in an era when black and white people were often segregated.

When one customer complained about having to sit next to black diners, Clifford's lengthy response concluded by stating that, 'It is our duty to serve all who enter our doors and conduct themselves within their legal rights. If the "ruin" so often predicted is around the corner, then we prefer to be ruined doing business in accordance with our obligations as a citizen. This is our policy. We survive or perish according to which point of view has greatest appeal to the people. Somehow we have faith in the people.'

In 1944 Clifford founded Meals for Millions after teaming up with a biochemist and a chef to create a high-protein, low-cost food supplement called Multi-Purpose Food (MPF) that was distributed to people in 129 countries.

The 'pay what you like' policy eventually became unsustainable and now the building in Downtown LA is a nightclub/restaurant/ venue space, but a big neon sign saying 'Clifton's' still graces its grand exterior. While Clifford passed away in 1969, his name lives on as a man who fought against poverty, prejudice and corruption.

AND FINALLY...

In 2014, Silo became the world's first 'zero waste' restaurant. This means everything from the furniture to the plates is made with recycled materials. Silo originally opened in Brighton on the south coast of England, and five years later relocated to London. In 2021, the restaurant received a Michelin Green Star for Sustainability and it has maintained that status ever since.

CHAPTER THREE

SEE YOU

INNO

LATER,
VATOR

A HAMMY DOG STORY

———

Innovation comes in many forms. In 2009, Australian entrepreneur Mark Murray made culinary history, of sorts, by becoming the first person to get a patent for a hamburger. But this was no ordinary hamburger, it was the Hamdog.

The hotdog runs through the middle and on either side is the burger, in between a hybrid of a sub and a burger roll.

Seven years later, Mark launched his product in the USA. It prompted comedian and talk show host Jimmy Kimmel to question America's place in the world.

'This country was built on hamburgers and hot dogs!' he proclaimed. 'By not inventing the Hamdog first, we got beaten, quite frankly, by people who can't get their toilets to flush in the right direction. Are we even allowed to call ourselves America anymore?'

'We used to be innovators. Who put cheese in a spray can? We did! Who put jelly in the same jar as the peanut butter so you wouldn't have to open two lids? We did!'

Fellow talk show host, comedian and satirist Stephen Colbert called on all American scientists to 'Drop what you're doing right now! I don't care what it is, combine lamb chops with a Slurpee, pipe gravy into a Twinkie, put cheese on anything that doesn't have cheese already – good luck finding it – because in the words of Robert F. Kennedy, some men see things as they are and say "why?" Others see things that never were and say, "I'd put that in my mouth".'

In the pantheon of food items that should never have happened, choosing the worst is a matter of taste. For everyone who thought the Cronut was the surest sign that Western civilization was in terminal decline, it was named one of the top 25 inventions of 2013 by *Time* magazine and has proven to be more than a passing food fad. The same, thankfully, cannot be said for Oscar Mayer's Ice Dog, a hot dog and mustard-flavoured ice-cream sandwich, which had us checking that it wasn't an April fool's joke. Or how about the General Food Corp's Jell-O for Salads, which came in four flavours: celery, Italian salad, mixed vegetables and seasoned tomato, all of which were said to be awful.

THE COOLEST INVENTION

The World Health Organization estimates that preventable diseases kill around 2.5 million people each year, half of whom will be aged under six. If this doesn't give you pause for thought, then consider that 85 per cent of potentially lifesaving vaccines are rendered useless in the last mile of their journey.

For vaccines to work they must be kept at a temperature range of between 2°C and 8°C (35–46°F) until use, but they are often exposed to extreme heat while they're being transported inside basic cool boxes (like the ones used to keep a four-pack of lager slightly chilled) to remote parts of the developing world, as well as during the immunization process. UK-based scientist Kitty Liao has designed an altogether different type of cool box, which could save thousands of lives.

Since she first developed the idea in 2016, Kitty's cool box (known as SMILE – for SMart last-mILE) has won a string of awards. When Kitty presented her invention at the Expo Live event in Dubai back in 2021, she caught the attention of Bill Gates.

He said that the cost of producing SMILE would comfortably exceed the price of a regular cool box. Kitty had the perfect retort, arguing that when you consider how many lives it could save, along with the many millions that are spent and wasted on vaccines that perish in the heat, the cost was relative.

'The creation of life-saving vaccines is well-funded, but too little has gone into the most critical last mile. It is now time to make that change,' she said.

'YOU'RE GONNA NEED A BIGGER BOAT'

———

The *Sjevik* was a Norwegian trawler that would scour the Barents Sea that lies between Russia and Norway in search of fish. In 1976, it landed a big one. A really big one. So big that it dragged the 1,000-ton trawler for about a mile. Then its identity became clearer, as a periscope emerged from beneath the sea. The *Sjevik* had caught a 360-foot [110-metre] nuclear-powered hunter-killer submarine of the Soviet 'November' class.

November submarines had become infamous for being stupendously rubbish. One sank off the coast of England in 1970 and they were easy to detect because they were so noisy. According to one Norwegian naval officer, a November would made a sound 'like the flushing of an antique toilet'. Therefore, the incident with the *Sjevik* provided yet another entry in the submarine's hall of shame.

Once it had become disentangled from the trawler, the sub and its crew beat a hasty retreat towards Murmansk in Russia.

'I guess they weren't too eager to talk with us,' said *Sjevik* skipper Ivar Hamnen. 'After all, it's pretty dumb when a modern submarine gets caught up in a fish net.'

AND FINALLY...

As failed inventions go, TwitterPeek reached the summit of pointlessness. It was a hand-held device devoted purely to Twitter and displayed up to eight tweets on its homescreen but only the first 20 characters of those tweets. Then you had to click on the individual tweet to read more. That was bad enough. Somehow Twitter thought people would part with $200 to do so much less than they could on their mobile phone. Tech and design website Gizmodo summed it up best in the headline for its review, which read, 'The TwitterPeek Is So Dumb It Makes My Brain Hurt'.

AN INNOCENT MAN

For eight months the cloak of suspicion hung over American Frank Rubio like, well, you can insert your own metaphor here.

In 2023, Frank became the first astronaut to live in space for more than a year – 371 days in total. He was only meant to be there for six months but his mission was extended to fix a coolant leak from a Russian Soyuz spacecraft, his mode of transport into orbit.

While he was up there, he took part in a live chat and thought it would be cool to show the audience the first tomato ever harvested in space. Having done his 'show and tell', Frank recalled, 'I was pretty confident that I Velcroed it where I was supposed to Velcro it... and then I came back and it was gone.'

Frank maintained his innocence, but somehow his achievements became almost secondary to the case of the missing tomato. Such is life. Then, later that year, the evidence turned up.

Fellow astronaut Jasmin Moghbeli cleared Frank's name and revealed the tomato had been found, or at least some of it. Eight months spent banging around a space station had taken its toll on the fruit. It had all but perished, but Frank's reputation had been restored.

AND FINALLY...

There are thousands of pieces of junk hurtling around in space, mostly made up of dead satellites. It's a serious problem and governments have been spending millions on finding ways to clear up the mess because it will become increasingly difficult to find pathways for launching new satellites. But there is also the debris left over from previous space missions, ranging from a spatula to a tank of ammonia roughly the size of a family fridge. At the end of 2023, if you had a half-decent telescope and looked in the direction of the International Space Station you would also see a bag floating in its vicinity. Loral O'Hara and Jasmin Moghbeli (again) were on a spacewalk when they let their tool bag slip to float aimlessly in space. But before anyone could say 'Louis Vuitton, we have a problem...' NASA said the bag would be vaporized when it eventually reached the Earth's atmosphere.

MY STORY
Mike Lawton

Based in Oxford, UK, Mike Lawton is an award-winning 'space entrepreneur'. He explains why what happens up in orbit could

help to tackle some of the biggest challenges faced by mankind on planet Earth:

❝I guess it's a bit of a cliché, but I grew up on a diet of *Star Trek* and *Doctor Who*. So, I was always fascinated with science fiction and space. And I'm old enough to remember when *Star Wars* came out at the cinema. Seeing that as a little boy, I was mesmerised. I wanted to be a spaceship captain, but then reality kicked in.

If I couldn't fly a spaceship, then maybe I could get into designing the stuff that goes into space. I thought, okay, you can make a satellite, literally the size of a shoe box, and have the same functionality as something that was the size of a truck ten years ago, but you still have to communicate with planet Earth. So even as satellites were getting smaller, their antennas had to stay at a fixed size.

There needed to be a new generation of antennas that were going to be price-compatible and physically compatible with these small satellites that could fold and maximise stowage efficiency.

The European Space Agency told me I was mad when I pitched the idea, which I took as a good sign!

Eight years later Oxford Space Systems, the company that I founded to make those antennas, was ranked as the most valuable UK start-up in the space industry. Space also has the potential to tackle some of our biggest challenges.

Around 14 million tonnes of plastic pour into the oceans each year, destroying ecosystems, damaging natural capital, and inflicting suffering on coastal communities. Plastic-i is a start-up that won the inaugural Hack the Planet competition in 2021 and uses satellite data and AI to map floating plastics in oceans, rivers and lakes. The inventors behind Plastic-i want to make our oceans free from the harmful impacts of plastic pollution.

Another groundbreaking space business in development is built around analysing the health of plants. Our crops go off-colour, as we do, when they're unwell. The health of a plant, when it grows, affects how it reflects sunlight back to space. Using satellite technology we can work out not only that plants are not well but also what's affecting them. This will allow us to massively reduce the amount of fertiliser and herbicides we need.

One thing that stops us from readily having access to the internet from space globally at the moment is the cost of the ground terminals. They're still very expensive. It's a bit like the early days of the mobile phone when this thing that looked like the size of a brick would cost £3,000.

I'm also involved in a company called Sat Tracker, which has made a real breakthrough on the technology side to massively reduce the cost of ground terminal antennas. In developing nations, especially across India and Africa, the idea of running copper cable or fibre optics over thousands of kilometres [to gain internet access] simply doesn't make sense because of the sheer scale and cost. If that can be commercialised, then we're going to unlock the potential of high-speed internet connections in developing nations where there is no internet at the moment.

Everyday items ranging from camera phones to artificial limbs were originally developed for space exploration.

And when you start developing materials that can withstand the tough environment of space, they instantly become applicable to demanding environments on the Earth.

I'm a firm believer that we can overcome pretty much anything with a bit of intelligent thinking. **"**

AND FINALLY...

When Rifath Sharook was a child growing up in India he would spend hours looking at space through a telescope in the company of his father, Mohamed, who was a professor and scientist. As a teenager, Rifath joined India's Space Kidz programme and led the six-person team that designed KalamSat, the world's lightest satellite. KalamSat was named in honour of rocket scientist and former Indian president Abdul Kalam, and was successfully launched on 22 June 2017.

EUREKA!

———

American Thomas Edison is probably the world's most famous inventor, credited with giving us the light bulb, the phonogram (that's record player to you) and the motion picture camera. He once said, 'If we all did the things we are really capable of doing, we would literally astound ourselves.'

On 30 June 2015, Lincoln Lowell Wood Jr overtook Edison as America's most prolific inventor, having filed 1,085 patents. Even at the time of writing, Lincoln is 82 and still filing patents.

Some of Lincoln's ideas have been a bit 'out there', including a laser-based shaver and a microwave oven that could adjust its temperature in response to different foods. He is perhaps most famous for the 'Star Wars' programme that was supposed to shoot down any Russian missile attacks from space, cost billions and never actually worked.

Yet Lincoln is mostly obsessed with trying to make things better for mankind and finding ways to tackle disease, famine and climate change. His ideas have included loading the skies with tiny particles that act as mini-reflectors, blocking out sunlight and cooling the Earth, as well as trying to design a laser that could kill mosquitos and wipe out malaria. Not bad for somebody who once said that in early teenhood he 'didn't do well in any classes'.

American entrepreneur Doug Evans loves beansprouts and regularly posts videos about their benefits, but he is best known as the man behind Juicero. It is often said that the best inventions solve a problem or fill a gap in the market. Juicero did neither. Launched in 2013 by Doug, aka the self-styled 'Steve Jobs of Juice', $120 million was invested in Juicero, a machine that squeezed its own packets of diced fruit and veg into juice. Initially, it entered the market costing $700, but soon the price came down to $400. What squeezed the life out of Juicero was a report by Bloomberg in 2017, which explained that you could extract the juice from the packs quicker by hand than by spending $400 on the machine. Investor Doug Chertok said, 'I have no doubt that they'll be very successful'. The company folded within months.

DRIVEN TO SUCCEED

An annual event in France, Le Mans is the world's most famous endurance motorsport event. Before 2012, only 55 cars could take part in the 24-hour race. Then Garage 56 opened, a berth made available for one car that 'explores the automobile technology of tomorrow and beyond'.

In 2016, the lead driver for the car that occupied Garage 56 was Frédéric Sausset. Four years earlier, Frédéric had picked up a rare infection while he was on holiday in the south-west of France. It spread rapidly, resulting in Frédéric losing all his limbs.

Astonishingly, he used this indescribable course of events as fuel to his fire, to fulfil a lifelong ambition and drive in the 24 Hours of Le Mans.

The car, an adapted Morgan LMP2, was designed in such a way that Frédéric could operate a throttle and braking system with his thighs, while his right arm limb was attached to the steering column.

The car could also be adapted to allow a non-disabled driver to take the wheel. Not only did Frédéric and his co-drivers complete the race but they finished 38th overall. 'At the time, I said to myself that if I managed to complete the 24 Hours of Le Mans, I'd set up a special programme for drivers with disabilities, to give them a chance of racing at the highest level, which would be a world-first,' Frédéric remarked.

He was good to his word. Six years later, he set up his own team that raced out of Garage 56, with two disabled drivers, Nigel Bailly of Belgium and Takuma Aoki of Japan, which finished 32nd overall.

Speaking to *Motor Sport* magazine, Nigel said, 'All we have been trying to do is to remove the stereotype of guys with disabilities racing'.

MAKE ROOM FOR THE MUSHROOMS

―――

The Green Alley Award was founded in 2014 to publicize and celebrate the best European start-ups in the circular economy, 'where the value of products, materials and resources is maintained in the economy for as long as possible, and the generation of waste minimized'.

The winners for 2023 picked up the first prize of €25,000 for reasons that went beyond the product.

S.Lab created an alternative to polystyrene made from hemp stems and mushroom roots (mycelium). The packaging is waterproof, 100 per cent biodegradable and decomposes in 30 days, which is impressive enough.

S.Lab's founders are both Ukrainian and when war broke out there in February 2022, they had to flee the country, initially settling in Hungary, then moving on to Italy, followed by Denmark, before eventually being offered the chance to set up their operation in Spain.

They hope to return to their homeland one day, but for now they are concentrating on developing their invention with global brands including L'Oréal, Samsung and Sony.

'All our team in different parts of Ukraine woke up to the sounds of explosions and all of us had to leave everything behind and evacuate to save the most basic thing – our lives,' said S.Lab co-founder and CEO Julia Bialetska.

'In just a few weeks, when all of us were in safe places, we went back to our start-up and understood that no matter what we still want to carry on, build and develop packaging materials to build a better future for all of us.'

QUESTION TIME

———

After Olivia Bland tweeted about an interview for a job at Web Applications UK, she was invited on to BBC radio to talk about her experience.

Olivia explained that the company's CEO, Dean Craig, adopted what he thought was a 'cruel to be kind' approach. He told her she was an underachiever (she had recently graduated with a first-class degree) and then brought in two other women to watch as he picked apart her application and belittled her. Olivia was offered the job but, understandably, turned it down. Dean later apologized for his behaviour.

At some point in recent history, the process of getting a job through sending in a CV and covering letter, followed by two interviews about 'what you can bring to the role', and 'where do you see yourself in five years' time?' was no longer considered to be adequate. The modern business world decided to get creative and turn the job application into a hellscape of multiple interviews, questionable tasks, and ridiculous questions, such as...

Google – Candidates for senior roles would be asked questions including 'How many piano tuners are there in the world?', 'Why are manhole covers round?' and 'A man pushed his car to a hotel and lost his fortune. What happened?'

(The answer is, he was playing Monopoly and lacked the money to pay the rent on the hotel location that his playing piece – the car – landed on.)

Zappos – The family-owned online shoe and clothing retailer preaches ten core values known as the Zappos Family Mission. Number three in that list is Create Fun and a Little Weirdness. And so when some unsuspecting applicant simply wanted to get a job to pay the bills, they probably didn't expect to be asked 'On a scale of one to ten, how weird are you?'
Top tip: If you still want to work there, then don't say one or ten.

Meta – Back in the day when it was known as Facebook, and to many people it still is, the global head of recruiting would ask candidates, 'On your very best day at work – the day you come home and think you've got the best job in the world – what did you do that day?'

Just taking a wild stab here, but one assumes that asking Mark Zuckerberg 'How is the metaverse coming along?' probably wouldn't be the right answer.

MAKING CLAY WHILE THE SUN SHINES

———

Jugaad is an Indian expression that has several interpretations, one of which is solving problems in an economical way. A good example of *jugaad* is the MittiCool refrigerator designed by Mansukhbhai Prajapati.

Mansukhbhai survived the earthquake that hit Gujarat back in 2001, although it decimated his plate-making factory. Many lives were lost, and some towns and villages lost their power supply, while there are plenty of other places in Gujarat that have never had access to electricity.

Mansukhbhai is a potter by trade and he came up with an ingenious invention: a fridge that is made out of clay, which is biodegradable and doesn't require any electricity. It operates best in a dry and hot climate. Water is poured into the upper chamber of the fridge, which then filters down and, as it evaporates, creates a cooling effect. This means that in the event of an emergency, the fridge will still work.

MittiCool was one of the inventions championed in the book *Frugal Innovation: How to Do Better with Less*. In an article published by Cambridge University, the book's co-author Professor Jaideep Prabhu said, 'It is human ingenuity that drives innovation – just like Mansukh Prajapati and his clay fridge – seeking opportunity in adversity, doing more with less, being flexible and simple, and following your heart.'

How do you create light in a dark room without electricity? Another example of frugal innovation is Liter of Light. Discarded plastic bottles are filled with a mix of water and bleach. They are then fitted into the corrugated metal roofs of homes in impoverished communities, where they refract solar light to provide interior daytime illumination without the need for electricity. Families can then save money to spend on lighting, cooking and hot water during the evening. More than 145,000 households in the Philippines use Liter of Light. Worldwide, that figure comfortably exceeds 350,000 in over 15 countries, and women-run Liter of Light cooperatives operate in the Philippines, India, Bangladesh, Pakistan and Colombia.

FROM SMALL PENCILS A MIGHTY SEED MAY GROW

The Sprout pencil is a pencil that can be planted after it's become too short to use, growing into herbs, flowers, vegetables and even spruce trees.

The owner of the company that produces the pencil is Danish entrepreneur Michael Stausholm. 'It is made from biodegradable graphite, to write with. But instead of throwing it away, you simply plant it in a pot,' he explains.

'It has a capsule at the end where you would normally have the eraser, and inside that capsule you have seeds.

'The first time you water it, the capsule will dissolve. From there you will just have to take care of it like any normal plant – water it, expose it to light and so on – and eventually those seeds will sprout up.'

Michael first saw the product on Kickstarter in 2013; it had been created by a group of students at the Massachusetts Institute of Technology (MIT), USA. 'I liked the idea of something as old school as a pencil that you could plant after use,' he says.

He then bought the patent. Initially, however, sales were slow and a close friend told him, 'I think you need to get a real job'.

Michael was stressed, tired and starting to question whether he'd made a big mistake. 'Then I thought, I believe in this, I want to do this, and I can do this.'

The Sprout pencil started getting press coverage and that coverage began to snowball. Then, in 2018, Michelle Obama used the product to help promote the publication of her bestselling book *Becoming*. To make the business more sustainable, 12,000 trees have been planted in Poland and one tree can produce 175,000 Sprout pencils. By September 2022, 50 million units had been sold worldwide.

'It's also about inspiring other people to look at products and think, "Okay, if you can take a pencil, and you can plant it instead of throwing it out, what other products can you re-use in different ways?" Because the biggest challenge we face today is not how we produce our products – it's how we dispose of them.'

Things took off again when the company started posting videos on TikTok. Although it did prompt some curious responses, including, 'Does it grow into a tree of pencils?'

BEERS TO YOU, JOHN HATCH

1000 Londoners is a series of film shorts made by UK-based Chocolate Films to show a different side of the capital.

'One of my favourite stories is that of John Hatch,' says Chocolate Films co-founder Mark Currie. 'In 2006, Youngs Brewery announced it had sold The Ram in Wandsworth to property developers. This is the site of Britain's oldest brewery with records going back to 1533. John was stunned that this crucial part of British brewing history was going to be lost, and offered to keep it going as a nanobrewery and constructed it all from spare parts, while the property developers were waiting to get permission to build on the site.'

Such is John's commitment that on one occasion he walked 14 miles [22.5 kilometres] in the snow to get to the brewery and ensure that it continued producing beer every week.

'The site has been used regularly as a filming location; guests to the brewery have included the cast and crew of famous TV dramas including *Silent Witness,* who used to drink John's Autopsy Ale,' adds Mark.

'John is still there, but now he works for Sambrook's, the brewery that became the site's new owner. When we asked him "What do you miss when you're away from London?", his answer was "the beer".'

JUST ADD WATER

———

'Imagine a world with skin cancer treatment that is accessible to everyone, regardless of their circumstances. A world where people don't have to worry about needing to pay thousands of dollars to get the treatment necessary for their survival, a world of equity and accessibility. That's the vision I've been working on for this past year. And I'm delighted to show you how one idea has the power to save millions of lives.'

This was Heman Bekele's pitch to become America's Top Young Scientist for 2023. And when we say young, he was a 14-year-old student from Annandale, Virginia. He won the competition by developing a soap designed to treat low-grade skin cancer, beating nine other finalists as young as 11.

Heman was raised in Addis Ababa, Ethiopia, and he became concerned about the number of people being exposed to searing heat, putting them at risk of getting skin cancer.

His soap would cost around 50 cents per bar, compared to the average cost of treatment, which is around $40,000.

'When first hearing about this issue, I was devastated by the number of preventable deaths caused by this illness and knew I had to take action,' he explained.

Heman wants to create a non-profit that can take his soap and distribute it among the communities that could not otherwise begin to think of paying for specialist treatment. His long-term ambition is to 'have made a positive impact on the world through my work and personal endeavours'.

WHERE THERE'S MUCK...

W indhoek in Namibia is home to a project that was set up in 1968, which could help the planet address its water-shortage problems, although the solution may, at first, turn your stomach.

Windhoek's population grew at such a rate during the 1960s that it soon became unsustainable, leading to a chronic lack of water. Then a group of scientists and engineers came up with an idea to address the problem. The Goreangab Reclamation Plant is where they 'clean' the sewage to filter out and eliminate the chemicals and all-round awfulness, and turn it into drinking water, all in just 24 hours. So, why aren't other cities around the world doing the same? Well, you have to get over the idea that the water you are drinking was once something you wouldn't go anywhere near.

Yet increasingly this is a solution either being considered or implemented in cities and states around the world, including California, USA. There is the old saying 'Where there's muck, there's brass' but in the future that could become 'Where there's muck, there's water'.

PURE SHEDONISM

———

In 1997, George Shields built the first motorized garden shed in South Derbyshire, UK. The idea came about by luck rather than design. He'd been asked to organize a pony and trap (carriage) for a friend who was getting married. But when he couldn't find one of those, George decided to improvise.

He had a 6 by 4 foot [1.8 x 1.2 metre] garden shed and also owned a quad bike. He realized the shed would fit perfectly over the bike and even added five hanging baskets. The shed could hit a top speed of 55 miles [88.5 kilometres] per hour and George classed it as an 'agricultural vehicle'.

George was a trailblazer for people like Kevin Nicks, who currently owns the world's fastest shed. Kevin had an old Volkswagen Passat and spent £5,000 building the framework of a shed around it, then started entering it into races.

Kevin explains the shed gets frowned upon by the classic car fraternity, who think it can't be legal, but he has the documents to prove it.

Simply known as Fastest Shed, it weighs 2½ tons and yet reached a record speed of 96.8 miles [156 kilometres] per hour while on a journey from Land's End to John O'Groats to raise money for a hospice in 2017. The following year, Kevin broke the speed barrier of 100 miles [160 kilometres] per hour. He revealed that the shed is part-fuelled by nitrous oxide, which makes it go so much faster. Nitrous oxide is, of course, also known as 'laughing gas'.

AND FINALLY...

TV presenter and mechanic Edd China has been the holder of world records for the fastest bed, fastest electric ice-cream van, fastest office desk and the fastest toilet. He also had the fastest shed until Kevin Nicks came along and broke his record.

CHAPTER FOUR

TREAT

WITH K

PEOPLE

NDNESS

ODE TO MARY JOY

———

During the great British heatwave of 1976, the fire brigade needed extra staff to cope with forest fires. Mary Joy Langdon went to her local station in Brighton, signed up and made the headlines as Britain's first professional female firefighter.

In 1983 she left the fire service to join the Church and became one of the Sisters of the Infant Jesus in Wolverhampton. Then, six years later, Sister Mary Joy moved again, this time to west London to set up an urban pony centre, surrounded by busy A-roads and high-rise estates, within walking distance of the original BBC Television Centre and Wormwood Scrubs prison. For over three decades the centre has transformed young people's lives, but maintaining a site for 21 horses and ponies in London is expensive.

The centre also runs art classes for people to paint the animals. One day in 2003, Mary Joy handed a man a book on how to sketch ponies. She had no idea that he was Lucian Freud, one of Britain's most famous artists, and Lucian enjoyed the anonymity. He passed away in 2011 but left a sketch of one of Mary Joy's ponies, called Goldie. When the sketch was sold in 2018, it fetched £40,000, paying for some much-needed repairs to the centre.

In 2024, Sister Mary Joy Langdon stood down as CEO of the Wormwood Scrubs Pony Centre, bringing to an end the latest chapter in an extraordinary life. 'The Pony Centre is a hidden gem and I always describe Wormwood Scrubs as a "rural oasis",' she said.

'Our main work is with young people who are disabled or have learning difficulties. We also have kids who come here from the local community, and they're as important as everybody else. We give hope to those who perhaps don't have many opportunities. Quite a few have gone on to work in the horse industry. It's not for everybody. They've got to want to be with the animals. But the centre has been so beneficial to so many young people.'

AND FINALLY...

Ebony Horse Club is located in the most unlikely of places, by a railway line next to a set of high-rise estates in Brixton, but it has become a haven for young riders in one of the most socially deprived parts of London. In particular, riders with neurodiverse conditions often find that they connect with the horses and that can have a transformative effect on other areas of their lives. 'One of our older riders was on the autistic spectrum,' explained the club's former general manager Naomi Howgate. 'He struggled to communicate, even with his mother, along with forming any sort of relationship with his teachers and other kids at school.

'But from coming to Ebony he started to build up trust with the horses. At first, he was very shy but then he learned he could trust another living being. His mother says the difference it has made at home is staggering.'

OUR STORY
Ali Catterall and Elise Burns

Ali and Elise (aka Kitty Collins) are the UK-based authors of *Kindness: A User's Guide*. Ali is co-director of the film *Scala!!!*, while Elise is a publisher. Together they produced a book that served as a definitive guide to kindness at a time when it was much needed for both the writers and their readers.

❝ Ali: We wrote the book at the end of 2020, during lockdown. Writing about kindness during those times served as the best tonic, a magical panacea for everything happening to us. I say 'us' because I had only recently connected with my biological family. It was such a privilege and a gift to write about that subject at that time.

Elise: On the day that we signed the contract to write the book I was diagnosed with breast cancer. Distraction is the wrong word, but it was just nice to work on this book and take my brain somewhere else. A year later, I got to ring the 'chemo bell', which marks the end of cancer treatment.

Ali: It would have been easy to do a twee book. It was also a flex against #bekind, in which those who are most often wielding that hashtag are doing it with an iron wand. It was also important to make it as inclusive as possible, encompassing gender, sexuality, ethnicity...

In the introduction I wrote, 'Kindness takes many forms. Within these pages are remarkable examples of humanity and acting for the greater good. All of them testament to the fact that where love isn't always possible, kindness always is.'

Elise: We could have written a whole book devoted to acts of kindness during Covid. Instead, we featured 52 people and acts, one for each week of the year, along with quotes and random facts. There were certain people we immediately wanted to include, like Dolly Parton and Bruce Springsteen. Also, there was Prince. Most of what he did never became public until after he died and we'll never know the full extent of his philanthropy. There is a wonderful quote from Chanhassen local Raisa Elhadi, which is where Prince lived. She said, 'Financial support was only a fraction of what Prince gave us... his real gift to Chanhassen was a lesson: be colorful, be passionate, be glamorous, be unapologetic, and above all, be yourself.'

Ali: It was the same with George Michael. So many stories came out after he died, some of which we knew when we were writing the book but the extent was astonishing. And he did it so discreetly, unassumingly, and with no hidden agenda. In the days immediately following his death, stories surfaced about his tipping debt-ridden barmaids many thousands of pounds. Another report [said] that he'd helped out anonymously at a homeless shelter, swearing fellow workers to secrecy.

Elise: We also featured some incredible stories about community. One is the relationship between Ireland and the Choctaw Nation (in Oklahoma, USA); an amazing, beautiful, reciprocal relationship between two nations that are so strikingly different but also have so much in common and are there for each other when they need it most. In 1847, at the height of the Great Hunger, the Choctaw Nation gifted Ireland $170. It wasn't the biggest donation, but it was the most significant. Choctaws are Native Americans who had been forcibly moved from their land, they had virtually nothing. The Irish never forgot it. It was absolutely lovely that they were donating thousands to the Choctaw Nation during Covid, because Choctaw people had one of the highest infection rates in the world and many people suffer from asthma or diabetes.

Another amazing story revolves around Hancock Bank, in Mississippi, USA. Hurricane Katrina destroyed the bank's head office and around 40 branches. In the aftermath, employees collected money from waterlogged banks, casinos and cash machines...

Ali: ...they then washed all the money, ironed banknotes and were literally laundering it but they gave it to anyone who needed it and set up an IOU system because there were no computers to log any information.

Elise: The bank gave out around $42 million and received virtually all of it back. They were short by $300,000.

Ali: I think we need stories that shake us out of our complacency. You know, things are magical, things are bizarre, things are peculiar because life is. You can find magic in a dustbin. It depends where and how you look. **"**

WILL THE REAL BILL NOVAK PLEASE STAND UP?

———

I t reads like a set-up for a movie and, depending on your age, the star could be Rick Moranis, Will Ferrell or Kevin Hart.

When Will Novak received an email inviting him to Angelo's bachelor party in Vermont, USA, he didn't recognize the sender and could have ignored, deleted or reported it as junk. Instead, he replied.

'I do not know who Angelo is,' Will wrote. 'I am a Will Novak, who lives in Arizona. Vermont seems like a very far way for me to travel for the bachelor party of a guy I've never met. That being said, count me in.' Will is a former comedian and clearly saw the comic potential.

The email was intended for Bill Novak who lives in Brooklyn and is friends with Angelo Onello. Will didn't expect a response, but the party organizers were so pleased with his message that they urged him to attend anyway. Will set up a GoFundMe page to cover the costs, and it substantially exceeded its $750 target.

When Will arrived at the airport in Vermont, he was greeted with six cases of beer, donated by a local brewery. He also found that the rental company had upgraded his hire car to a $75,000 Maserati.

Later that evening, a drunk man got into his vehicle and drove off. Will's heart sank, but he didn't call the police and his faith was repaid when the car was returned soon after; the drunkard had simply 'wanted to take it for a spin'.

And just to add to the feelgood nature of the story, Will and Bill became friends. 'Dozens of people, maybe even hundreds, have said things along the lines of, "Well, the news cycle is so depressing, people are deeply upset by what they see on the news, and this is so stupid and so funny,"' said Will.

AND FINALLY...

In 2014, Taylor Swift posted a video titled 'Surprising Gena'. Taylor had received an invite to a wedding from superfan Gena Gabrielle, and although she couldn't make the big day, the invite also included the bridal shower. 'I've never been to a bridal shower, so we are going to fly to Ohio today', says Taylor.

That's not all. At the end of the video, there's a message for Gena that says, 'Thank you for inviting me to your bridal shower, and for inviting me into your life since 2007!!!'

DOUGHBALLS WITH EXTRA DOUGH

F our months after opening Frankensons pizzeria in Las Vegas, USA, owner Frank Steele was struggling to shift enough slices, wings and fries to make ends meet. Unbeknown to Frank, one of his staff tried getting a reviewer in to help drum up business.

The first critic/influencer that was contacted wanted $2,600 to do a review. The next one, however, said he didn't charge and paid for his own food. The reviewer then turned up on the first Monday of 2023 and would transform Frank's business overnight.

Speaking on local TV channel KTNV, Frank said, 'I like to ask my customers, "Where are you from, what do you do?" And he quietly said, "I'm a food critic."' But this was not just any food critic. It was Keith Lee, who has over 16 million followers on TikTok, and Keith often makes a point of reviewing small independent eateries that may otherwise be ignored.

He didn't just like Frank's food, he loved it. Keith's online review racked up 10 million views in just four days, while Frank went from barely having half a dozen customers a day to having queues around the block. Keith returned four months later and the food was just as good (except for the lemon pepper wings, apparently). Meanwhile, Frank took on extra staff to cope with the demand. When asked to reflect on what that single review had meant to him, Frank's response was 'life-changing'.

AND FINALLY...

You can order fried tarantula at the Romdeng restaurant in Phnom Penh, Cambodia, but that isn't what makes this restaurant remarkable. Well, actually it sort of does, but its purpose goes far beyond trying to freak you out with fried insects. Romdeng is a non-profit. Its dishes are cooked and served by young adults who have lived on the streets, and they receive training in hospitality, food service and management. For what it's worth, your author recommends the fish amok and the beef stir fry with red ants.

ANOTHER (LEGO) BRICK IN THE WALL

The pandemic made 18-year-old student Charlie Jeffers from California, USA, consider the situations of kids and teenagers who are less fortunate.

He grew up playing with Lego and said it helped him to understand and learn maths, as well as art and engineering concepts; it can also boost cognitive development.

Charlie also knew that when kids grow up, Lego often gets discarded and ultimately ends up in landfill sites. So, he founded Pass the Bricks. Charlie takes in any unwanted Lego bricks and sets, and washes and repurposes them so they can be handed to other kids and families who can't readily afford to buy toys.

He has managed to enlist the help of more than 20 volunteers, has collected well over 900 pounds of Lego by weight, and has distributed more than 3,000 repurposed sets made from leftover pieces, with titles like 'Superman Would Like One Day to Sleep In' and 'Iron Man Goes to the Car Wash'.

When Charlie isn't putting together Lego sets or studying or doing taekwondo (he's a black belt), then the chances are that you'll find him beekeeping.

He has helped to produce hundreds of jars of honey from a beehive in his family's garden that have raised thousands of dollars for SchoolsRule-Marin, a local charity that promotes educational equity.

'What an exceptional young man to have recognized the importance of helping others at such a young age. He should serve as an example to us all!' said SchoolsRule-Marin executive director, Trisha Garlock.

YOU CAN CALL HIM, AL

———

During 1997 and 1998 a climatic weather pattern known as El Niño resulted in a series of torrential downpours in California, USA, back in the day when that sort of thing very rarely happened.

Alfonso 'Al' Nino was a resident of Nipomo, a small town 11 miles [18 kilometres] from the Californian coast. You may be able to guess where this story is going, especially as he was listed in the phone book as 'Nino, Al'.

He ended up receiving 100 or so calls from random people either blaming him for what had happened or asking why he wanted to make it rain?

That would have tested the patience of most people, but not Al, who was a retired naval pilot. Instead, he decided to embrace the collective madness that had gripped his callers, to do what many of us would love to do but wouldn't dare. He simply played along.

'I told one man who'd called me to ask me to stop the rain that I'd stop it for him. He called me three days later to thank me for making the rain stop.'

'I've rather enjoyed it,' he added.

BRING YOUR WOK TO WORK

———

Born in India in 1954, Pinky Lilani CBE DL has been the driving force behind the Women of the Future Awards and Asian Women of Achievement Awards. In 2018, she helped to establish the Leading Lights campaign, which each year recognizes 50 people who exemplify kindness and leadership. Those leaders can be anyone from a small business owner to the CEO of a multinational – even former Liverpool football club manager Jürgen Klopp.

Pinky is also a prominent spokesperson for people with disabilities, having been profoundly hard of hearing for over 20 years, and relying on hearing aids. What's more, she is always in demand as a public speaker and her talks are often built around the theme of kindness. There is another reason, however, behind why Pinky is so popular, and that's because she brings her wok to work.

'People love creativity, innovation and drama,' she says. 'Some years ago, I was asked by the University of Cambridge Judge Business School to be a speaker for their Global Leaders lecture. They had the head of Barclays [bank] the week before, whereas I was running a small company. Why would a bunch of MBA students want to hear me speak? So I said, "Can I bring my wok?"'

Pinky often addresses her audience while making her signature dish of Bombay potatoes. 'You may say, where's the connection between cooking and leadership? But you need fresh ingredients, passion, sometimes you need to turn up the heat… I love it because nobody else does it. And hopefully, people remember that.'

WHEELS OF FORTUNE

When Adam Ely's daughter was working for Domino's Pizza in Oklahoma City, USA, she would always get a lift to work from one of the delivery drivers.

Adam is a disabled war veteran – he was previously a helicopter mechanic with the US Army – and his hobby is fixing up cars. He could hear that the delivery driver's car was in serious need of ragging service but the driver couldn't afford to stop working. Adam offered to do the job for just $75, instead of the $450 she had been quoted by another mechanic, which was the going rate. 'That's when I had the lightbulb moment, that we could affect some change with very little effort,' he said.

Along with his wife, Toni, Adam founded Hard Luck Automotive Services, a non-profit repair shop in Oklahoma City, USA. They help people who don't have the means to fix a car on their own, but for whom having a set of wheels in working order is about more than getting from A to B, it is about keeping a roof over their heads.

As long as the customer has the parts, Hard Luck will provide the labour. Since it was founded in 2017, Adam and his team have helped over 4,000 families.

Hard Luck relies on public donations but has garnered so much goodwill that when the lease on his lot was about to expire in 2021, city officials handed over a plot of land to Adam free of charge, enabling him to build a new site that keeps Oklahomans on the road and out of trouble.

0800-SANTA-CLAUS

———

The red phone on the desk of Colonel Harry Shoup of the Continental Air Defense Command (CONAD) started ringing. It was 30 November 1955, and the world was in the grip of the Cold War.

'It's either the Pentagon calling or the four-star general, General Partridge,' Shoup assumed, recalling the moment years later.

'Yes, sir. This is Col. Shoup.'
No response.
'Sir? This is Col. Shoup.'
Nothing.
'Sir, can you read me all right?'
'Are you really Santa Claus?'
'Would you repeat that please?'
'Are you really Santa Claus?'

Realizing the call was almost certainly genuine, albeit to the wrong number, Harry said he was indeed Santa.

Legend has it that an advert had been placed in the *Gazette* newspaper in Colorado Springs by Sears, Roebuck and Company with a number to call Santa, but one of the digits was wrong.

And that's the version of the story that gets shared every December. Without wishing to destroy the magic of Christmas, in 2014, Matt Novak, writer for the tech website Gizmodo, revealed that a young girl did make that call but she got two numbers the wrong way around, which took her through to Harry's regular line, and he didn't pretend to be Santa.

But that misdial inspired Harry to start what would become a Christmas tradition, involving millions of phone calls from around the world. On 23 December 1955, a press release was put out to say that 'Santa Claus was assured safe passage into the United States by the Continental Air Defense Combat Operations Center here which began plotting his journey from the North Pole early Friday morning,' adding that, 'CONAD, Army, Navy, and Marine Air Forces will continue to track and guard Santa and his sleigh on his trip to and from the US against possible attack from those who do not believe in Christmas.'

So, the Santa Tracker was born. CONAD then became NORAD (North American Aerospace Defense Command) and every year it brings in an army of volunteers to answer around 130,000 calls from kids asking about Santa's progress as he journeys around the globe delivering presents.

THE GIFT THAT KEEPS ON GIVING PART I

———

As Ian Jones says in the foreword for this book, a lottery win is the sort of story that can go from an 'and finally...' to the day's biggest event.

In 2019, Frances and Patrick Connolly from Hartlepool, UK, landed a EuroMillions jackpot.

Recalling the moment it happened, Frances said that Patrick had told her, 'We've won'.

'Yeah, but we've won what?' she replied. 'I thought he was going to say £1,000 or something.'

'No, you're misunderstanding me. We've won.'

A couple of expletives later I said, 'You must be joking'. Patrick said he wouldn't joke about something like that.

The jackpot was £115 million.

'Then all the conversations about "What would you do if..." went out of the window. We said nothing for 10 minutes.'

She added, 'This is a massive sum of money and we want it to have a huge impact on the lives of other people we know and love as well as on our future too. It's going to be so much fun giving it away,' she said. 'The pleasure for me is going to be seeing people's faces.'

The Connollys decided they would hand over half of the money and set up a fund to give away a certain amount each year. Three years on from that win and Frances said they'd already exceeded that annual figure by ten years.

'I'd have been a millionaire anyway if I took back all the money I've given away over the years, she told PA News, adding, 'If you're stupid before you get it, you're going to be stupid afterwards'.

'If I had any advice for a winner... I'd say money liberates you to be the person that you want to be.'

THE GIFT THAT KEEPS ON GIVING PART II

———

Doing a good deed, in the expectation that the recipient will, in turn, do another good deed for somebody else is known as 'paying it forward'. Its history dates back centuries.

If, for example, a neighbour brings around a jar of coffee, instead of paying them back you would make a similarly kind gesture towards another neighbour.

In 2020, during the pandemic, groups of women known as the Sisterhood of the Traveling Wine (a take on the book and film adaptation *The Sisterhood of the Traveling Pants*) sprang up across America.

The way it worked was that 'wine fairies' would collect addresses and those people who signed up would then be asked to knock on somebody's door, leave a gift, which could be alcoholic or non-alcoholic, and then run for the hills. Or behind a bush.

Cara Rindell brought the movement to Raleigh, North Carolina. 'It's all about bringing others happiness and making new relationships,' Cara told the *Good News Network*. 'It starts off as a random act of kindness to a stranger and becomes a friendship with the neighbour you didn't know you had.'

Tracy Murley founded the Sisterhood of the Traveling Wine group in Canton, Michigan. Speaking to *Good Morning America*, Tracy said, 'We get so lost in everything we do every day and running kids here and there and everywhere and we get so competitive. I think this has really united our community and opened us up to where we're willing to know our neighbour. Maybe it took a pandemic to get us here, but let's not lose it.'

AND FINALLY...

55 burgers, 55 fries, 55 tacos, 55 pies, 55 Cokes, 100 tater tots, 100 pizzas, 100 tenders, 100 meatballs, 100 coffees, 55 wings, 55 shakes, 55 pancakes, 55 pastas, 55 peppers, and 155 taters. The Netflix comedy series *I Think You Should Leave with Tim Robinson* features a sketch called 'Pay it Forward' in which Robinson tries to pull a scam at a drive-thru by offering to pay it forward to the man behind him, before circling round

to get back in the queue so that the 'previous' man has to pay for his order of 55 burgers, 55 fries, etc.... The line instantly became an internet meme.

AQUA THERAPY

———

Chris Antao is the founder of Gnome Surf, a unique surfing club in Rhode Island, USA. The club serves over 3,000 athletes and families, and Chris says, 'Over 95 per cent of our athletes either have autism, Down syndrome, ADHD, depression, or anxiety.'

Among those athletes are 15-year-old twin boys Kash and Hollis Palumbo. Speaking to PBS, their mother Margaret said, 'They were diagnosed at 15 months of age with autism, and a handful of other diagnoses. Both of my boys are pretty much non-verbal. Hollis is non-verbal; Kash has some language. These are kids that typically do not get invited to birthday parties or sleepovers. To see them having fun doing something that typical kiddos do, it's a feeling like no other.'

Abby MacCurtain suffers from a mitochondrial disorder, which means that whenever she goes out with her mother, Heidi, she is confined to her wheelchair, except when they go to Gnome Surf. 'To give all the control away and watch it, it was so enjoyable – her smile, her laughter, and everybody around her – it was awesome. And we couldn't wait to have another opportunity to do it,' said Heidi.

Chris understands the challenges faced by neurodiverse kids and has battled throughout his life with ADHD, depression and anxiety. The work that he does together with the rest of the team at Gnome Surf is almost like a form of therapy for him.

CHAPTER FIVE

ANIMAL

HOUSE

THE TRIAL OF THE CENTURY

I n 1984, one of the more extraordinary trials in the recent history of the British legal system began at Snaresbrook Crown Court, Essex, UK, and was eventually settled at Bow Street Magistrates Court in central London.

John Sewell was a police constable who, along with his wife, was the proud owner of a tomcat called Marmaduke Gingerbits. Not so, according to Monty Cohen, who lived on the same road. Cohen said he was the real owner of the cat, which had gone missing and was, according to Cohen, called Sonny.

When John went round to see Monty and claim what he said was his – the Sewells' cat had disappeared when they were on holiday, while he was being looked after by a family friend – one of Monty's associates intervened, claiming he was a black belt in karate, and then began fighting John.

While the dispute was being settled in the courts, the cat had to remain in police custody (actually, it was a local cattery), and it was escorted by an officer to the hearings.

When Monty was summoned to be cross-examined at Snaresbrook, he got into the dock, immediately looked at the cat, and shouted 'Hello Sonny!' Meanwhile, when John told the judge the cat was named Marmaduke Gingerbits, the judge gave a withering response: 'Marmaduke who…?'

Eventually, the case went to Bow, where the Sewells produced a devastating piece of evidence – a smoking saucer, if you will – that would ultimately decide the destiny of the ginger tomcat.

They said the cat had an allergy to milk. A representative from the RSPCA then appeared in court to support that claim, and so Marmaduke Gingerbits was returned to his rightful home and a dairy-free diet.

'THAT ONE'S FOR YOU, CODY'

C ody Dorman from Richmond, Kentucky, USA, was born with Wolf-Hirschhorn syndrome, a rare genetic disorder that affects many parts of the body. Doctors told Cody's parents that he would only live for a couple of years, but having defied that prognosis, Cody's story would become known to a wider audience because of his association with a racehorse.

In 2018, the Make-A-Wish Foundation organized a trip for 12-year-old Cody and his family to Gainsborough Farm in Kentucky, which is home to some of the best thoroughbreds in the world.

An unnamed six-month-old foal struck up an immediate affinity with Cody. Then the pandemic struck, but once restrictions were lifted, Cody immediately expressed his desire to return to Gainsborough Farm. Again, there was an instant bond between the teenager and that very same horse. When asked why there was this unique connection, Cody, communicating via a tablet, said, 'Because he found me, and he hasn't forgotten me. We have the same heart and drive. We never give up.'

And so, the horse was named Cody's Wish and he went on to finish third in each of his first three races before Cody asked his parents if he could watch his horse run at the track for the first time. Cody's Wish duly won and didn't stop winning, securing an entry into the 2022 running of the Breeders' Cup Dirt Mile, a race that's worth $1 million.

As the runners entered into the home stretch it was a two-horse race between Cody's Wish and Cyberknife. It was nip and tuck up the straight until Cody's Wish put his head in front in the final strides. As he crossed the line, legendary race caller Larry Collmus cried, 'That one's for you, Cody!'

A year later Cody's Wish won again at the Breeders' Cup, following another photo finish in the final race of his career. Cody was there to see it, but he passed away on the journey back from the racecourse. He was 18. His parents, Kelly and Leslie, said, '... we were determined to help Cody live his best life for however long we had him. Anyone who has seen him at the racetrack, especially around Cody's Wish, understands that in many ways, he taught us all how to live, always keeping a positive attitude and being more concerned by those around him than himself.'

MY STORY
Sharon Walia

Sharon is a journalist and filmmaker based in the UK. Her second movie, *The Keepers of the Pigs* was released in November 2023 and is utterly unique. She explains how a film about guinea pigs came about because of an 'And finally ...' story that went viral and took her around the world...

    ❝ Around six years ago I met Brendan Woodhouse, a firefighter from Nottingham, who would go out to Greece and take part in search and rescue operations to save refugees trying to cross the Mediterranean Sea. That became the subject of my first film *The Movement* as I joined him on a four-week-long rescue mission.

I came across Brendan because I was a reporter, mainly covering the Nottingham area. I did a lot of social justice stories about homelessness, poverty, and migration. On the flip side, I also did stories on wildlife and animals. When I first started doing TV news for *Nottingham Live*, there was always a competitive streak among the reporters to get the lead story.

That changed very quickly. We soon realized it was the 'And finally...' story at the end of the news that viewers tended to remember.

I've got three guinea pigs as pets. I bloody love guinea pigs! But I had no idea that a sanctuary existed in Nottingham until I went there to do a piece about Avalon Guinea Pig Rescue, which is run by Sharon 'Shaz' Kelly.

We then put the story online with a clip to go with it. The next day I came into work, my editor showed me the analytics on Twitter and Facebook and said 'Sharon, your guinea pig story has gone viral. People are watching it in India, the Philippines, Mexico, Peru...' I thought, 'There's something in this.'

I've since become friends with Shaz and I asked, 'Would you be up for being in a documentary about guinea pigs?' She looked at me and said, 'It's about time!' All of which led me towards making *The Keepers of the Pigs*.

Every film needs a narrative; in this case it is Shaz and her attempts to keep Avalon going.

We went to a guinea pig show in Birmingham and all you could hear was the sound of hair dryers. It turned out that it was competitors grooming their guinea pigs. I met Pete Wardman, a builder and former amateur rugby player. He had no interest in guinea pigs until he went to a show with his wife and got the bug. He became a guinea pig judge, and it has enabled him to travel the world because British judges are revered wherever they go.

Then I went to the biggest guinea pig show in France with Jme Eglington, who is a hairstylist and a tournament judge. There was this intense conversation with the French about what is the best shampoo for guinea pigs. The answer, in case you're wondering, is Herbal Essences because it doesn't contain sulphates.

I couldn't make the film without going to Peru, but it was on the red list during Covid so everything was put on hold for two years. Eventually, I contacted Napoleon, who runs the country's largest festival, where people sing songs dedicated to their guinea pigs.

Napoleon opened so many doors and introduced me to Carmen and her husband, Ulises, two professors who are eco ecologists. What they discovered is that guinea pig poo is stronger than methane but without the damaging effects to the environment. So, they are using it as an alternative source of energy to power homes.

The strangest thing, given the status that the guinea pig has among Peruvians, is that they are also served as food. As a vegan, trying to get my head around that was difficult. Then I also discovered producing guinea pigs helps to lift the women who breed them out of poverty.

In Doncaster, I visited Cavy Corner (*cavies* is the Latin word for guinea pig), a rescue centre, shortly after one of the owners, Winston Tate, had passed away. He was a local legend and was buried in a guinea pig-inspired coffin.

The film also highlights issues around welfare. When the series *Fleabag* was launched in the USA, Amazon Studios recreated Hilary's, the guinea pig café from the show, in Los Angeles, which had the unforeseen consequence of people getting guinea pigs as pets that then went on to be abandoned or neglected. We also explored the history behind animal testing; 'guinea pig' is part of our vocabulary because of experiments carried out on animals.

Some people have asked me, 'Why guinea pigs?' The thing that people don't get is that each one has their own distinctive character. They are so much more than a pet, and I hope that's what people get from seeing the film. "

IT WAS A PIG OF A WEEK

——

On the morning of 8 January 1998, a lorry pulled up at an abattoir at Malmesbury, Wiltshire, UK. As the driver started unloading his live cargo, three Tamworth pigs made a dash for freedom. Two of them evaded capture as they burst through a fence, swam across the River Avon and went on the run. Or should that be trot?

The journalist who broke the story was Wendy Best of the *Western Daily Press*. She was told about the escapees following a routine morning phone call to the local police station – something that she did as a matter of course.

The tale was then picked up by a news agency and subsequently featured on *News at Ten* as its 'And finally...' piece – and that's when the story went global. The pigs became known as the Tamworth Two.

Part of the reason it captured the imagination of news crews as far away as Japan and New Zealand was because of the animated film *Babe*, the story of a pig that escapes from becoming a farmer's Christmas dinner. The film was released in 1995 and became a worldwide hit.

Here, suddenly, we had a real-life Babe – or Babes. The pigs, who were brother and sister, became known as Butch and Sundance, after the famous American outlaws.

Also, being January, and just a few days after people had gone back to work following the holiday season, the timing was perfect for a good-news story to lift the early-year gloom.

The pigs evaded capture for almost a week by hiding out in a thicket, but were eventually caught by a local butcher, who handed them over to their owner, Arnoldo Dijulio, a local road sweeper. Arnoldo said he still intended to send them to the slaughterhouse, until the *Daily Mail* intervened, offering him an undisclosed sum of money to let Butch and Sundance ride off into the sunset. Actually, they were taken to Kent, to see out their years at an animal sanctuary.

AND FINALLY...

There were several postscripts to the Tamworth Two, the best of which centered on the hunt for Arnoldo. The media spent days trying to find him, but what they didn't know was that every morning he would sweep the road right outside the hotel where all those reporters were staying.

BIQUETTE – THE G.O.A.T.

While Butch and Sundance lived out their lives in peace and tranquillity, the opposite could be said of Biquettte, also known as the Punk Rock Goat.

When she was aged five, Biquette (which is French for 'young female goat') was going to be sent to the local abattoir because she could no longer produce any milk. Instead, people running a community farm in Mauriac, a village in south-west France, stepped forward and said they would take her in.

The farm had a barn where groups would come and play gigs and Biquette was free to walk around the venue as she pleased. Apparently, she didn't take much interest in the groups that played there, except one. Wormrot is a grindcore group from Singapore who play very fast and very loud punk music, and when they came to Mauriac, they got the goat's attention.

A picture of her standing at the front, between the band and the mosh pit, was taken sometime around 2012. And she stayed there for the duration of their set, which included an impromptu song/noise performed in her honour. The picture went viral and the legend of Biquette was born.

A SPIKE IN THE HEDGEHOG POPULATION

—————

It was only a few years ago that hedgehogs were listed as an endangered species in the UK – their numbers have dropped by a third since the start of the millennium.

One of the reasons is a lack of connectivity – either because of hedgerows in rural areas, or garden fences in urban areas.

Hedgehog Street is a campaign run by the People's Trust for Endangered Species and the British Hedgehog Preservation Society (BHPS) to encourage communities to help their local hedgehog population thrive.

One example is Dale Road in Keyworth, Nottinghamshire, which has become known as 'hedgehog highway'. In 2020, residents got together and put 40 holes in walls and fences so that hedgehogs could roam freely from garden to garden.

Dale Road subsequently won the award as Britain's Biggest Hedgehog Street in 2022. Not only has the 'highway' brought the community closer together, but it will also help secure a spike in the local hedgehog population.

AND FINALLY...

In 1995, a 'toad tunnel' was built in Davis, California, USA. Despite the name, it was designed to allow frogs to go under an overpass. The community fully embraced the idea, with the local postmaster creating a 'toad town' outside the entrance. They thought of pretty much everything, except that frogs didn't want to use it.

PAWSOME REUNIONS

REUNION NO. 1

Kerry Smith is a photojournalist who works for the NBC 5 channel in Dallas, Texas, USA. In 2022, Kerry made the news himself, or rather it was his dog, Jazzy.

In 2015, Jazzy ran away after being spooked during a Fourth of July fireworks display.

For the next seven years, the Smiths tried to find Jazzy but to no avail. Then one day, Kerry received a call from Orange County Animal Services in Florida. They had found Jazzy in a hotel room in Orlando, about 800 miles [1,300 kilometres] away, but they had been able to trace her owner because she had been microchipped. It was made clear to Kerry that Jazzy was in a poor state but he got on the first flight from Dallas to Orlando for an emotional reunion.

'My message to everybody is to chip your dog,' Kerry told NBC 5. 'I knew as soon as she went to a vet I would get the call I've been waiting for for seven years.'

A spokesperson for the rescue service said, 'We have to endure heartache and heartbreak every day. Every now and then though, we get to watch something like this, and it makes every minute worth it.'

REUNION NO. 2

In 2011, the Crandalls who live in Glendale, Arizona, USA, adopted a three-year-old Bichon Frise and named him Minion. 'He was a super cute little Bichon. Very playful. He would sleep with my daughter, Callie,' said Skip Crandall.

But after a workman had a left gate open Minion disappeared, and when it has been 12 years since you've last seen your dog, you've most likely written off all hope that you will ever see him again.

Then Skip's wife, Raleigh, received a string of calls but couldn't return them because she was in the middle of teaching a class full of kids. So she forwarded a voicemail to Skip. The message was left by Alyssa Sanford, an animal control officer from Maricopa County. She said, 'Hey, I have this dog. His name is Minion. If he's yours, call me back.' He was picked up as a stray around 10 miles [16 kilometres] from where the Crandalls live.

Alyssa had no idea that Minion had been missing for so long – 12 years is the average lifespan of a dog. When she spoke to Skip, Alyssa had to make it clear that Minion was now 15 and showing clear signs of age. But when she arrived at their house and Minion was reunited with his owners, 'instantly his body language changed'.

Minion sadly passed away soon after the reunion, but he got to spend his last days back with his owners.

REUNION NO. 3

One newspaper headline described it as 'The Cross Country Canine Caper'. Petunia the pit bull went missing from her home in Spotsylvania County in Virginia, USA, shortly after Thanksgiving in 2003.

Her owners, the Pruitt family, put up posters, placed ads in newspapers, and visited dog pounds, but it seemed as if their dog had simply vanished, never to return. In 2011, Meg Eden was driving along a remote rural road outside Sacramento, California, USA, when she saw a stray dog.

Petunia's microchip was traced to a vet who then contacted the Pruitts.

'And I said where has she been found, and she said Sacramento, California,' recalled Kristin Pruitt. Indeed, that is one hell of a journey, clocking in at around 2,800 miles [4,500 kilometres] – roughly the distance from London to the North Pole.

As Kristin said, 'I can't believe she would've trekked across the Mississippi, to the Rocky Mountains, and the Grand Canyon, to get to California on her own.'

AND FINALLY...

In 2019, the Fargo Brewing Company in North Dakota, USA, teamed up with 4 Luv of Dog Rescue, a local animal shelter, and started printing pictures of dogs for adoption on its cans. In the following year, the Just Pizza & Wing Co. restaurant in New York took the concept a step further when its owner, Mary Alloy, who is also a volunteer with the Niagara Society for the Prevention of Cruelty to Animals, posted pictures of dogs available for adoption inside their pizza boxes. Any diners who adopted a dog would receive a $50 voucher for the pizzeria. Sales immediately doubled, although surprisingly they didn't change the menu to add a Pupperoni option. Sorry ...

WHAT SHALL WE DO WITH A DRUNKEN MOUSE?

Jerez de la Frontera in Spain is the home of Tio Pepe, one of the world's most famous brands of sherry. At González Byass, the company that owns the Tio Pepe wineries, they faced a big problem in the shape of little mice nibbling away at the huge casks kept in their cellars. The bosses planned to bring in a cat until workers, who had grown quite fond of the mice, apparently threatened to go on strike.

One of those workers had noticed that when the mice sipped away at any droplets of sherry on the cellar floor they became too drunk to focus on the casks. To this day, a feature of any guided tour of the Tio Pepe cellar is the sight of a tiny ladder that leads up to a small glass of sherry left out for the mice.

I AM THE WALRUS

On New Year's Eve 2022, Scarborough Borough Council in the UK cancelled its plan for a fireworks display for health and safety reasons. The explanation, which was widely supported by residents across this seaside town in Yorkshire, was because of a walrus on the latest leg of his European tour.

Thor the Walrus started playing to audiences in the Netherlands, then moved on to Dieppe in France, before wowing the good folk of Calshot Beach in Southampton, and then he headed up the east coast for a stop-off in Scarborough.

To put the rarity of such an occasion into context, according to the Natural History Museum, there had only been 27 sightings of a walrus on British shores in the 130 years before Thor's arrival.

Thor's sojourn in Scarborough was short-lived and was followed by a special guest appearance at the Royal Northumberland Yacht Club in Blyth, before turning up in Norway two months later in Breiðdalsvík, Iceland. It turned out that he had quite a discerning palette, as he turned his tusks away from the frozen fish being tossed to him by the locals. Only the freshest fish will do for Thor.

Given that, at the time, Thor was thought to be somewhere between three and five years old, weighing in at just 1,650 pounds [750 kilograms] – a mere youngster, given that a walrus can live up to 40 years and grow to 4,000 pounds [1,800 kilograms] – who knows where he may turn up next...

Before Thor, there was Benny the beluga whale. In 2018, Benny was spotted splashing around in the River Thames in the UK when his natural habitat would be in waters around the Arctic Circle. At first, people were delighted to see a white whale, but then experts explained that belugas are highly social animals and there were worries that he was lonely. Yet, Benny spent three months in a stretch of water around Gravesend before he disappeared. A spokesperson for British Divers Marine Life Rescue told the *Daily Telegraph*: 'It probably has moved on. We don't know where it went, because we don't know where it came from!'

SWANNING AROUND

E very year at the beginning of November, the swans that reside in the city of Lakeland in Central Florida, USA, are given a physical check-up. They have a special significance because they are descendants of swans that were given to the city by Queen Elizabeth II on 4 February 1957.

The first swans appeared in Lakeland in 1926. They became pets for residents who had winter homes there, and soon the city formed a Swan Department to oversee their wellbeing. But Florida's waters are also home to big and dangerous predators. By 1954 there were no more swans.

A former Lakeland resident living in England took the matter to the Queen, as the royal family are the owners of all mute swans in the UK. The Queen duly responded by donating a pair of swans, who made the journey from the outskirts of London to Lake Morton, in the centre of Lakeland. Their wings were clipped to ensure they didn't fly away and become prey for alligators or crocodiles, and the swan population has thrived ever since, with the November 'physical' becoming an annual tradition.

HAIR TODAY, HAIR TOMORROW

———

Beth and Brian Willis from Newcastle, UK, made the *News at Ten* in 2008 wearing two jumpers made from the fur of their dearly departed dogs. Providing far more information than anyone necessarily needed, Brian later told the *Evening Chronicle*, 'They are extremely warm and pretty much waterproof. Unless it is banging it down, it is fine. I've always got a sweat on by the time I get from the bus to the shops.'

Beth added, 'Some people think it's disgusting but it seems normal to us. They go through the wash just like ordinary clothes and they last forever.'

It's not so disgusting to Jeannie Sanke, who has turned garments made from dog hair into a business. Knit Your Dog was founded in 2014 and, as Jeannie's website states, 'Knitting dog hair is nothing new, believe it or not!'

AND FINALLY...

The official term for wool spun from dog hair is 'chiengora'. Yes, chiengora is a thing (*'chien'* is French for 'dog', and the 'gora' part comes from 'angora'). It was apparently coined in 1993 by Annette Klick, a spinner from America.

THE BUTTERFLY COLLECTOR

———

Tim Wong is an aquatic biologist who is also known as 'the Butterfly Whisperer.' For as long as he can remember he has been fascinated by the insect. Upon discovering that one particularly rare species, the California pipevine swallowtail, was under threat of extinction in his native San Francisco, USA, Tim decided to take action.

He learned that the butterfly only feeds on one plant, the California pipevine, which had all but died out as the area became more urbanized. He went to the San Francisco Botanical Garden, the only place in the city where you could still find the plant, and they gave him some clippings so he could grow pipevines at home.

Tim then created the perfect environment in his backyard – one that would allow the butterflies to eat new crops of the plant, and then mate, breed and ultimately thrive. That process started in 2012. By 2017 he'd developed thousands of butterflies and single-handedly saved the species from extinction in San Francisco. The butterfly itself is a sight to behold, evolving from an orange-speckled caterpillar into a beautiful flying insect covered in shades of blue. Tim told the *San Francisco Chronicle*, 'I didn't realize how much people appreciated our native butterflies until I started to share it more broadly on social media. We have these beautiful, incredible animals and native plants that are worth preserving, even in a developed environment like San Francisco. People can make a difference.'

DESERTING RATS

———

An infestation of rats is every tenant and property owner's worst nightmare. That also extends to the wildlife that populates small islands around the world. Rats historically travelled the globe as stowaways on ships, and if they decided to get off at an island, or deserted a sinking ship, then they could rapidly become the dominant species and treat local seabirds as prey. This, in turn, could have disastrous consequences for coral reefs that rely on guano (aka bird poo) as a nutrient.

In 2022, a programme was set up on Irooj, in the South Pacific Marshall Islands, to rid the islet of rodents. It took a year, but eventually conservationists could declare Irooj a rat-free zone, which means that over time other species will begin to appear.

'The island feels alive again,' said Kennedy Kaneko, the Republic of the Marshall Islands National Invasive Species Coordinator. 'Careful monitoring showed zero signs of rats on Irooj. In fact, seabirds and crabs were found in abundance.'

AND FINALLY...

After rats were successfully eradicated from Rábida Island in the Galápagos, a tiny gecko appeared and the species has thrived ever since. Before that, any evidence of a gecko on Rábida was linked to sub-fossil records going back more than 5,000 years.

A TALE OF TWO PERCYS

———

Some 40 years ago a racing pigeon called Percy was featured on the TV news when he was meant to set off on a journey from Penzance to Manchester in the UK (a distance of 330 miles [530 kilometres], as the pigeon flies). Instead, he ended up going from Penzance to Halifax... Canada (2,600 miles [4,200 kilometres], give or take). At the time it was reported that Percy had flown all the way, but given that racing pigeons have never been recorded flying further than approximately 1,000 miles [1,600 kilometres], that seemed pretty unlikely/impossible.

It just so happened that around the same time, the Royal Yacht *Britannia* was passing through Penzance, where a pigeon had flown on board and hitched all the way to Halifax, Nova Scotia.

AND FINALLY...

In 2012, another racing pigeon, also called Percy, was meant to be en route from Fougères in France to Cannock in Staffordshire in the UK, but also ended up in Canada, albeit this time 600 miles [965 kilometres] further west in Quebec. Fortunately, Percy eventually ended up living with a Canadian family who loved pigeons.
His mode of transport? According to his previous owner, Bernard Chambers, he had, in all probability, hitched rides on several ships.

'SAY HELLO TO MY LITTLE FRIENDS...'

———

Little Friends was a community farm in Pontypridd, Wales, that hit the headlines in 2000 when a male guinea pig named Sooty managed to tunnel under a fence and into a compound of female guinea pigs.

'We knew that he had gone missing after wriggling through the bars of his cage,' said Carol Feehan, who ran the farm. 'We looked for him everywhere but never thought of checking the pen where we keep 24 females. We did a head count and found 25 guinea pigs – Sooty was fast asleep in the corner.'

But having successfully found Sooty, nobody had considered the fact that he had made a lot of new female friends in a very short space of time, which probably explained why he was tired. According to Carol, 'all hell broke loose' when, around nine weeks later, 42 baby guinea pigs were born within two days of each other.

Thankfully she managed to find new homes for Sooty's sons and daughters just in time for Christmas. His story was reported around the world, and by Valentine's Day, Sooty had received 20 cards from as far afield as New Zealand.

THE ITALIAN STALLION

———

Whichever horses win this year's Epsom Derby, Kentucky Derby, Grand National or Prix de l'Arc de Triomphe, it is more than likely they will be related to a thoroughbred that was famously pictured in 1941, being led out of a bombproof stable in Newmarket, UK. Nearco won all 14 of his races, and you can trace the family tree of pretty much every great modern thoroughbred going back through decades to the horse known as 'the Italian Stallion'.

His trainer, Federico Tesio, sought permission from Italy's fascist dictator Benito Mussolini to run Nearco in the 1938 Grand Prix de Paris, and the idea that an Italian horse could beat the best from France and England clearly appealed to Il Duce.

It was only a week earlier that Nearco had won the Gran Premio di Milano, and his train journey to Paris took 36 hours. Even so, he duly finished first, much to the fury of the Parisians, after his jockey greeted the crowd by giving a fascist salute.

Federico then did a secret deal and sold Nearco for £60,000 to Martin Benson, an English bookie who traded under the name of Douglas Stewart and who was once name-checked in a George Orwell poem.

Il Duce was said to be furious, although Federico promised the dictator one of Nearco's offspring. Soon after war broke out in 1939, Martin paid for a bombproof stable to be built for his prized possession, to ensure that the horse could go on to sire hundreds of little Nearcos. That picture of Nearco being led out of his custom-made home soon became famous.

Nearco showed little interest in breeding and was virtually impossible to handle, going through ten stud grooms in as many months, so it looked like Martin had made an expensive mistake. Then he hired Ernie Lee, a groom known for his unique ability to connect with unruly horses.

When Nearco died aged 22, Lee was heartbroken and never worked with another horse. But the results had been astonishing. Frankel, Arkle, Secretariat, Nijinsky, American Pharoah, Kauto

Star, Black Caviar, Flightline, Winx and many more great thoroughbreds are all related to Nearco.

AND FINALLY...

When it comes to procreating, there has never been a greyhound like Low Pressure. He raced in England before becoming the most prolific sire of all time, with 3,000 offspring born between 1961 and 1969.

MIGHTY MOUSER

———

It is said that where there's barley, there's mice. Therefore, a whisky distillery needs a cat and Towser was a mouser the likes of which nobody had seen before. When the Guinness Book of Records visited the Glenturret Distillery in Scotland, she caught between three and four mice a day. When she passed away in 1987, they reckoned Towser had caught 28,899 mice over a prolific 24-year career – although granted, one could find fault in the methodology of assuming she always caught that many mice every day. There is a bronze statue of Towser outside the Famous Grouse Experience and she received the ultimate accolade in 2017 by having a bottle of whisky named in her honour.

CHAPTER SIX

THAT'S

ENTERTA

A LOT OF DOUGH TO GET STUFFED ON CRUST

———

I f you were pitching an idea for a film, it seems reasonable to assume that the story of a 7-foot [2-metre]-tall shrimp coached by a pub landlord to become a boxing champion wouldn't cut much ice, especially when trying to convince investors they should part with £100,000 to get it made.

Crust is a movie that pulls off the cinematic trick of being more ludicrous than it sounds, although it did star Naomie Harris (Eve Moneypenny in *Skyfall*) and Kevin McNally (Mr Joshamee Gibbs in the *Pirates of the Caribbean* franchise).

It never appeared in any cinemas, and didn't even go straight to video or DVD when it was released in 2003. None of which would have mattered to Guy Hands, who had gained a reputation as the best dealmaker in the City of London. Guy had been advised to invest in films guaranteed to fail because he made a 40 per cent profit via a UK tax loophole. But somewhere in between handing over £100,000 to make an atrocious movie and that movie getting made, the loophole closed and the story made the papers as Guy took his advisors to court.

'The reason I invested in the films was to obtain the benefit of the tax reliefs which would at least ensure I got my principal investment back,' Guy wrote in a prepared statement submitted to the court.

Ironically, the investors may have been better off releasing the movie in the UK. *Crust* would go on to become a cult hit in Japan, and it inspired several similar movies, including *The Calamari Wrestler*, *The Kung-Fu Cod* and *The Crab Goalkeeper*. Okay, we made up *The Kung-Fu Cod* but the other two genuinely happened, and *The Calamari Wrestler* was a box-office success.

AND FINALLY...

In *Crust* the protagonists plan to make their fortune by staging a man versus crustacean contest. Also in 2003, UK TV channel ITV planned to broadcast *Man versus Beast*, only for the show to be pulled.

The show's presenter was John Fashanu, who had previously been a professional footballer and presenter of the television show *Gladiators*. Stills from the programme show a strongman engaging in a log-rolling contest with an elephant.

The format was first broadcast in America, and it was going to be 'enormous'; viewing figures would 'go through the roof', said John. Instead, it was animal rights protestors who quite rightly went through the roof. In a textbook example of saying one thing and doing another, a spokesperson for ITV said, 'It was a scheduling decision and nothing to do with criticism of the show from pressure groups. We will reschedule it at a later date.' They never did.

DENNISES THE MENACES

In the UK, Dennis the Menace wears a red-and-black striped top, and has a dog called Gnasher. He was created by David Law for the world's longest running weekly comic, *The Beano*.

Then there is the American version created by Hank Ketcham that continues to appear in newspapers across the USA. Although the characters are quite different – the UK Dennis loves causing mayhem, whereas the US Dennis encounters trouble by accident, wears a black-and-blue striped top and has a dog called Ruff – they are bonded by an extraordinary coincidence.

In the UK, Dennis first appeared on 12 March 1951, the very same day the US Dennis made his debut in a newspaper comic strip. Yet neither artist knew what the other had done.

'DON'T YOU KNOW WHO I AM?'

———

The history of showbusiness is littered with stories of people who failed to convince members of the public, and even people within their own industry, that they weren't imposters.

The go-to story on this subject is when the real Charlie Chaplin entered a Charlie Chaplin lookalike contest at a travelling fair and finished in 20th place. Or he finished 27th and the event was held in San Francisco. Or he finished seventh and it was held in Germany.

Nobody can be entirely sure, because the story was first told by Lord Desborough, who had heard it from his wife, who had heard it from Hollywood star Mary Pickford, and it was never confirmed by the man himself. A report in *Newsweek*, which used the book *Hollywood Winners and Losers* as its source, then stated that Chaplin had indeed entered a competition in which he had finished third, but it had taken place in France in 1975.

There was no such confusion with Dolly Parton, at least not in terms of what happened and where. She was in Los Angeles and had found out that a bar was hosting a celebrity lookalike contest for drag queens. So, she turned up with a group of friends and later recalled that the competition was mostly made up of wannabe Chers and Dollys. The winner was the lookalike who got the most applause, but Dolly finished well down the field.

In 2011, former WWE superstar CM Punk was refused entry to Madison Square Garden, New York, where he was due to fight later that night. The doorman didn't believe he was a wrestler, even though he was the reigning WWE champion at that time, and one of the biggest stars in the ring.

The Real Ghostbusters was the animated spin-off TV series from the film *Ghostbusters*. In the movie, the character of Winston Zeddemore was played by Ernie Hudson. During an interview with *The A.V. Club* about his career, Ernie was asked the following question: 'This may be an urban legend, but did you audition to do the voice of Winston for the *Ghostbusters* animated series, only to be passed over for the gig?'

Ernie confirmed the legend was indeed true, but the story had an added element of ridiculousness. At the audition, the director didn't know who Ernie was and then, when the actor started reading the script, he was told that he was doing it all wrong. It needed to be more like what Ernie Hudson had done in the movie.

Not only did Ernie fail to get the part, but the voice of Winston Zeddemore was given to his friend Arsenio Hall.

CAN'T TELL YOUR RIGHT FROM YOUR LEFT

E very map of the world you look at is wrong; some continents are really far bigger, and some countries are much smaller than they appear to be on most maps. Africa is way larger than it looks – you could fit the USA, China, Greenland and Europe inside it. Yet even if the scale is wrong, at least the African nations are in the right places. Not so for the UK's *News at Ten*.

At one point in the early 1980s, the show's opening credits began with the screen rapidly zooming in on a satellite image of the world, and then the letters ITN (Independent Television News) would appear. The credits were seen every night by millions of people, but it wasn't until ITN received a letter from Dr John Townshend of the Department of Geography at the University of Reading that they realized something was wrong.

Dr John wrote, 'Given your undoubted accuracy in reporting facts, could you ensure West Africa appears on the left of my screen and East Africa on the right?' Somehow the image of Africa had been flipped so left was right, and right was left, yet nobody else had spotted it in around 500 broadcasts.

AND FINALLY...

In 2019, furniture company Ikea had to issue an apology when a map that it was selling was found to exclude New Zealand. This has been quite a common occurrence over the years and there is even a Tumblr page devoted to World Maps Without New Zealand. But this was especially embarrassing for Ikea given that it happened as the Scandi homeware giant was opening its first store in, well, you can guess the rest...

MY STORY
Chris York

Chris was a director at SJM, one of the biggest music promoters in the UK, and was best known as the man behind the Oasis 'mega-gigs' at

Knebworth in 1996. He passed away in 2024, following a long battle with cancer, but in the previous 16 years Chris had worked tirelessly as the promoter for the Teenage Cancer Trust gigs. One of those gigs made the headlines in 2013, but as Chris explained in this interview, the most important stories often happen behind the scenes...

" We've staged a lot of memorable gigs for Teenage Cancer Trust (TCT) over the years, collaborations that couldn't happen anywhere else. An obvious one was when Noel Gallagher walked out with Damon Albarn and they performed on stage at the Royal Albert Hall, just over ten years ago. If you wanted to have a perfectly written story for the reviews and the news, that was it. They'd finally grown up. Peace and love had broken out!

These gigs started in 2001 after The Who's Roger Daltrey was receiving medical treatment and got talking to a surgeon who was involved with TCT. Roger then offered for The Who to play a fundraising gig for the charity and it grew from there.

The group's promoter was Harvey Goldsmith who is best known for Live Aid, and he oversaw the TCT gigs for seven years. Then the opportunity came about for SJM to take over with Harvey's blessing. We built on the shoulders of giants, as it were.

It developed from a one-or two-night event to what is now seven nights at the Royal Albert Hall. I'm reliably informed by Mr Pete Townshend that the event has raised £30 million for TCT, and £23 million of that has come in the time that SJM has been involved.

Right up until the late 1990s, a teenage cancer patient would be placed in an adult ward, and that can be a very bleak existence. Our simple goal was to improve that situation, and the money we've raised has since gone to create more than 20 dedicated units for teenagers in hospitals. We have also become a model for a US version of TCT. And we're doing this at a time when there's a lot of pressure and a lot of criticism of the health system in the UK (unduly in my opinion).

The gigs always start with Roger's monologue that teenagers are pivotal to the world of rock and roll and pop, and therefore we should be doing whatever we can to ensure that a teenager with cancer should have as full and active a life as possible.

A lot of the customers and patrons of the event never see the deeper side of TCT but no stone is left unturned making sure that a teenager's day, or days, at the Royal Albert Hall is as memorable as possible. We have music workshops, and discussion groups, and virtually all the artists will join in. At the end of those workshops the young people get to perform their song and every person involved in putting on the shows will be watching. And we do that inside a very special and unique venue.

When it comes to booking the acts, there will be other charities that have relationships with artists so it's not always as simple as picking up a phone. I guess it's more of an art than a science, is what I'm saying, and I've got a small black book to call in favours when I need them. A lot of people that I've booked have basically agreed to do it because of my relationship with them and my unique powers of persuasion!

Often, they won't know much about the charity. It's important they understand our message whenever they're asked about it. We're not a medical fundraising charity, we're not trying to treat cancer, or develop vaccines, or groundbreaking new equipment.

We've had some very special shows, be it New Order, the Gallaghers in their various guises, Paul Weller, Robert Plant, Nile Rogers, Florence Welch, David Gilmour, Paul McCartney...

Getting the right balance, however, doesn't always quite work. Although we weren't involved in it, there is another gig that sticks in the memory from 2006. Judas Priest playing metal at the Royal Albert Hall for TCT was probably a step too far!

It's a chance for some acts to play in a venue that would be otherwise out of their reach. Some nights, you get a sense of occasion there that simply doesn't exist anywhere else.

And then we have what has become known as the 'selfie' moment when we get thirty teenagers with cancer to walk on stage just before the headliners perform. That took a bit of explaining to Dave Grohl and the rest of Them Crooked Vultures when they played in 2010.

But I think what that moment does is seal the bond between the people we are directly trying to affect the lives of, the audience, and the performers. "

APPETITE FOR DEDUCTIONS

F ollowing years of playing hard and partying way harder, Guns N' Roses bass player Duff McKagan was rushed to hospital in Seattle, USA, in 1994, and spent ten days on a ward with a burst pancreas. He was told by doctors that giving up booze wasn't merely an option – it was a matter of life or death.

While he was recovering, Duff found a new focus in life, and it was his tax returns.

He began to look through the band's financial statements but struggled to make sense of them. 'I didn't know how much we had made or lost on the tour.' Duff took a finance class, then enrolled at Seattle University to study accounting and business. Duff soon became the man other musicians turned to because he could articulate where their earnings were going – and usually it was straight to the record label.

As he's proclaimed, there's nothing more punk rock than making sure you get paid your dues after you've played a show and avoiding getting ripped off by 'the man'. Damn straight, Duff.

AND FINALLY...

Other rock stars to dabble in accountancy include Robert Plant and Mick Jagger. Meanwhile, as career changes go, try beating Lou Reed who, after quitting The Velvet Underground in 1970, took a job at his father's tax accounting firm as a typist earning $40 a week.

'PETER, YOU CAN DRIVE MY CAR. YES, I'M GONNA BE A STAR.'

Pete Saunders was the road manager for several groups in the 1960s but he was also the sort of bloke who would be brought in to make sure the bands turned up for their gigs and that they also got paid.

He became something of a right-hand man to some of rock's biggest stars too, including Rod Stewart, when he was the lead singer in the Jeff Beck Group, which also featured future Rolling Stone Ronnie Wood.

Because the band was always on the road, there wasn't much time to learn how to drive and take a test. Pete would drop the band off following a gig, but they were spread out in different parts of London and its suburbs. Deciding that he'd had enough of this, Pete said, 'Tell you what we'll do, I'll go and take your driving tests for you.'

Speaking to the UK's *The Big Issue* newspaper in 2018, Rod explained, 'These were the days before you had to have your picture on them. So he did. I think he took Woody's as well.'

And so Rod has never passed the test for a UK driving licence, but he did pass his own test when he moved to the US eight years later.

AND FINALLY...

Rob Mawhinney was the lead singer of Lights Over Paris, a group from Los Angeles that never achieved chart success, but he successfully pursued a rock 'n' roll lifestyle, which included a $750,000 customized tour bus. Rob did this by taking out huge loans based on false documents that stated he had $7 million in the bank. The real figure was closer to $10,000. Rob managed to get $11 million from four different banks, and they were willing to give him even more. This was all the more remarkable given that it happened between 2008 and 2011, just after the global financial crisis, when getting big loans was about as easy as performing keyhole surgery without being a qualified surgeon.

A LOAD OF POLLOCKS PART I

When Teri Horton walked into a thrift store in San Bernadino, California, in 1992 she spotted a painting on canvas. 'It was ugly. There was nothing to it,' she recalled. Nevertheless, she asked the store assistant how much it was, and got the reply, 'Gimme $8'. Teri haggled her down to $5.

A few weeks later, she put the canvas on display at a garage sale. A local art teacher saw it and told her, 'You might have a Jackson Pollock painting'.

Teri, a retired truck driver, had no idea who Pollock was, but then she discovered that if the painting was genuine, it could be worth tens of millions. Pollock died back in 1956 so she had to rely on a succession of experts to determine whether it was an original or not.

Some immediately dismissed it as an imitation, but others believed it was the real deal.

As she sought to authenticate the painting, Teri's story became the subject of a film, *Who the #$&% Is Jackson Pollock?*, which was what her response to that art teacher had been. She turned down an offer of $9 million from a Saudi art collector and set the price at $50 million. Teri passed away in 2019, with the painting locked away in storage. When she'd been asked if she thought it was worth the price that she was asking for it, her blunt response had been, 'Hell, no. It's worth the $5 I gave for it.'

A LOAD OF POLLOCKS PART II

———

Josh Levine used to run J. Levine Auction and Appraisal in Arizona, USA. In 2015 Josh visited a house in Scottsdale to look at some sports memorabilia. However, there was also a painting in the garage that Josh instinctively thought could be a Jackson Pollock. Yes, another one.

He then spent thousands of dollars tracing the history of the painting and getting it authenticated. Eventually, Josh put it up for auction in 2017, with a starting price of $5 million, although he was expecting to receive anything from $10 to 15 million. Then the story took a few dramatic turns. The auction was cancelled when several bidders failed to pass credit checks, and two years later, J. Levine Auction and Appraisal went bankrupt. But the painting was never declared among the assets. To this day, nobody other than Josh himself (and possibly a private buyer) knows what happened to the Pollock found in a garage.

AND FINALLY...

According to figures from national and international crime-fighting organizations, about 20 per cent of the collections in major museums around the world contain paintings that are not by the artist to whom they are attributed. In most cases, they will be forgeries.

THAT'S THE (NEW) WAY TO DO IT

Each year on the second Sunday of May, the garden of St Paul's Church in central London, UK, is filled with booths housing hand puppets, operated by people talking in a variety of different voices – high-pitched, nasal, whiny...

Welcome to the annual Covent Garden May Fayre & Puppet Festival, where Punch & Judy puppeteers from around the world gather to perform.

The garden is where Samuel Pepys, the diarist who documented both the Great Plague and the Great Fire of London, first saw and wrote about a puppet show featuring a character known as Mr Punch.

Those who are inducted into the Punch & Judy fellowship are classed as 'professors', a ritual that dates back to Victorian times. Among them is Josh Neville, currently the youngest professor, who makes his own puppets and first started performing in 2014 when he was six years old.

Josh has adapted his show for today's audiences, allowing Judy to stand up for herself.

'I think it's just traditional family fun that you can enjoy, for all ages, and that's what's kept it going really,' he says.

WHAT THE BUTLER SAW

——

O obah Butler is the writer and broadcaster who famously created a fictional restaurant called The Shed at Dulwich, London, UK, and got it to number one in Tripadvisor rankings for restaurants in the capital – ahead of 14,148 other eateries – through a series of fake five-star reviews.

When the story went global, Oobah became inundated with requests for interviews from news channels around the world. But whoever he spoke to about The Shed he found himself being asked the same questions – often the only difference between the interviewers was the accent. So Oobah came up with another ruse – to get a series of actors and models to stand in for him and see if anyone could tell the difference.

The first fake Oobah's interview failed because it was edited out of a piece by the BBC. But Oobah learned from his initial mistakes and coached subsequent fake Oobahs on how to give the answers that broadcasters were looking for. Fake Oobahs then made appearances on various TV channels and radio stations, while the real Oobah documented all of this to make a video about how he conned the media over a story about conning Tripadvisor.

A DEVILISHLY GOOD PRANK

———

During the process of removing the stalls for restoration work at Bath Abbey, UK, in 2018, two coins were found, each depicting a devil, with CIVITAS DIABOLI (city of the devil) written on one side and 13 MAJ ANHOLT 1973 (13 May, Anholt, 1973) on the other.

It was a reference to a series of incidents that took place on that date on Anholt, an island that lies between Denmark and Sweden.

Residents had found 'evidence of rituals', including bones tied together with string, masks and even a shrunken head.

One newspaper even went so far as to suggest there had been a human sacrifice and named the victim. Imagine their surprise when that person contacted the paper to say that she was very much alive and well.

At that point, the trail went cold and nobody could explain what had happened on Anholt. Then coins like those later found in Bath started to appear across Denmark, sometimes with letters apparently written by a satanic high priestess called Alice Mandragora. In addition, an outsized human tooth was sent to the director of Rosenborg Castle, home to the Danish crown jewels.

The mystery was eventually solved in 2013 by the Danish newspaper *Politiken* and the story became known as 'the prank of the century'.

The person behind it wasn't a high priestess called Alice but an art-gallery clerk called Knud Langkow who had died in 2004, seemingly taking his secret to the grave.

While Knud's colleagues were shocked, it transpired that other people had also been in on it, including the engraver who had made the coins, which were auctioned in 2020 with an asking price in the region of £100.

Knud's niece, Lene Langkow Saaek, said of him, 'I think normality annoyed him. He did not like ordinary.'

THE NAKED TRUTH

———

Ruth Liptrot has been a TV news reporter in the UK for over 20 years, covering everything from what is often described as 'hard news' to human interest stories. She is something of a go-to correspondent for 'And finally...' pieces.

One of her most memorable reports was back in 2007, when she covered the naked calendar girls.

Ruth explains 'The story behind it was that Kara Westermann-Childs' daughter, Rosie, has a severe form of autism. Kara set up a group called the Full Monty Girls, who performed burlesque shows to raise money for Rosie so she could go to a special clinic in Florida. But the treatment cost £17,000 a year. So, she came up with another fundraising idea and managed to get 100 women to strip off for a calendar in a field in Stroud, and I joined them.

'We did it on a Saturday, which was meant to be our day off, but it was a story that we wanted to cover. Obviously, there's the heartwarming aspect of what all these women were doing for Kara and Rosie, but then you've got the awkwardness and the comedy.

'It presented a number of challenges for the cameraman, Phil Bloom. He said every time he tried to get a shot we could broadcast, something would stray into the picture that wasn't suitable for a family audience. He thought it would be a fun story to do and it ended up being one of his most stressful!

'Right at the end I said to the camera that I couldn't strip off because I hadn't shaved my legs. But that was as much about the fact that Phil would see me naked. We're not just colleagues but also good friends.'

The story was then posted on YouTube, where it racked up 60 million views.

'A really important element of these stories is to generate genuine warmth,' Ruth adds.

'Often that can involve going on the street and conducting vox pops. It's one of those things that a lot of reporters don't like doing but I absolutely love it.

'On one occasion Liam Gallagher was about to launch his clothing range, Pretty Green, so the producer had this idea I should dress up and talk like Liam and ask people what they thought. Never mind that I was seven months pregnant at the time.

'The first man I went up to, I asked if he thought Liam was a style icon. He said, "I don't like him. He's rubbish!"

'There's this idea that a TV news report is about somebody talking to the camera, but really it's not. You need to know how to listen to people as well. We keep saying to trainee journalists that you shouldn't be writing the script before you film anything because you don't know what picture you're gonna get.

'But that is also what makes the job so wonderfully unpredictable and enjoyable.'

CHAPTER SEVEN

LAW AND

ORDER

PARKING YOUR TANK ON THEIR LAWN

Phillip Matton was so excited after finishing his driving lesson that he took the vehicle back home to show his parents. Back in 1983, Phillip was a 19-year-old soldier, and his mode of transport was a 42-ton [38-tonne] Chieftain tank that he drove 80 miles [130 kilometres] across two counties from Bovington Army Camp, Dorset, to Basingstoke, Hampshire, UK.

Or at least that's one version of the story. The other is that he was denied a weekend pass to see the folks, so he took matters (and the tank) into his own hands.

Either way, what we do know is that he parked the tank outside his mum and dad's house, only to find they were fast asleep. So, feeling a bit peckish, Phillip made himself an egg sandwich, as one does after a tiring journey by armour-plated instrument of destruction. Then he got back in his tank and went to school. Indeed, what better way to impress pupils and teachers at your former seat of learning than parking your tank on their lawn? Or, in this case, their playground.

By the time he'd arrived at Cranbourne School, Phillip was being followed by seven police cars. He handed himself over to the law, before being returned to Bovington where, presumably, he was given a lesson in the dos and don'ts of tank driving, among other things. When his dad, Anthony, was asked about the incident, he told reporters that Phillip was 'a home-loving boy and he came home to show us that he could drive a large tank. Unfortunately, we were in bed. This is not the sort of thing we would expect of him, but we still love him.'

PARKING YOUR TANK ON THEIR FESTIVAL

———

When the Welsh alternative rock band Super Furry Animals wanted to promote their single 'If You Don't Want Me to Destroy You', they could have done the obvious thing, which back in 1996 meant taking out an advert in the music papers. Instead, they bought a tank.

'We'd been in the pub with the band, and I think it was Daf [the drummer] who said they would like to put a sound system in a tank and drive it up The Mall [in London],' recalled John Andrews, marketing manager for the group's record label, Creation Records. 'So I said, "Well, I better buy you a tank, then."' He wasn't joking either. A few phone calls later, and John was heading off to an airfield on the outskirts of Nottingham to purchase a vehicle made from military grade steel for £10,000.

'Once we had the tank, we thought, "We need to do something with it". But when you take a tank to a festival, you're thinking, "What could possibly happen?"'

The band's new mobile, armour-plated sound system appeared at music festivals across the UK that summer and was also featured on Welsh TV news.

The tank made its debut at the ill-fated Beetle Bash Festival, in Stratford-upon-Avon. John was staying off-site, and when he left everything was in full swing. Between that point and when he returned, the event had run out of money. The atmosphere, which started off being a bit edgy, threatened to get out of hand. So, the band locked themselves inside the tank while feral festival-goers climbed aboard their temporary home.

'When I returned the following morning, the festival had gone. There was nothing left... except for the tank!'

Then the legendary music publicist and former manager of The Smiths, Scott Piering, suggested that there was some obscure law that would allow the band to park their massive armoured car outside BBC Broadcasting House and play 'If You Don't Want Me to Destroy You', as long as it was in the early hours of the morning.

'Everything I did with Super Furry Animals was brilliant. At the time, it didn't seem much different from everything else we were doing,' John recalled.

In fact, the following year John bought two 50-foot [15-metre] inflatable bears to go on tour with the band. The bears represented 'good' and 'evil', and the authorities got involved when the evil bear suddenly appeared in Primrose Hill, London.

John worked with some of the biggest British bands of the 1990s, including Oasis and Primal Scream, but Super Furry Animals have a special place in his affections. 'There's no marketing handbook in the world that tells you to go and buy a tank. We did it because it was fun. It was a privilege to work with them. But above all that, they are brilliant artists and songwriters. It was simply my job to help them realise their ideas outside of the music.'

AND FINALLY...

The story had another wonderful twist when, at the end of summer 1996, the tank had served its purpose and they wanted to sell it. Word had got back to John that Don Henley could be an interested party. That's Don Henley of the Eagles, who recorded the best-selling album in US music history. Why Don? John explained: 'Flogging a tank is not exactly the easiest thing to do, but we sold it to him because he collects military vehicles.'

THE CROWN VS JOHN TIMBRELL

Mention the name John Timbrell to magistrates and judges in Gloucestershire, UK, and you might get a few funny looks.

John, a retiree, has represented himself in numerous court appearances because, in his own words, he is 'a person who is extremely knowledgeable about the law.' Others might say that the evidence – and there's an awful lot of it – says otherwise.

Trial No. 1. In 2014, John was in court for assaulting a police officer and then trying to make a citizen's arrest on the judge. Verdict? Guilty. John was sentenced to 21 days in prison for contempt of court.

Trial No. 2. In 2018, John pleaded not guilty to obstructing a policeman while also admitting in court that he had indeed obstructed a policeman. He described the officers who arrested both him and a neighbour as 'badly trained dummies' who didn't know the difference between lawful and legal. He also went on to call the legal system the 'illegal system'. See what he did there. Verdict? Guilty. John was fined £850. 'Oh well, I half-expected it anyway,' he said.

Trial No. 3. John was back in court in June 2019 to appeal against his 2018 conviction. He made a series of legal claims that included his assertion that the conviction was no longer valid because he said so. Verdict? Still guilty.

Trial No. 4. In December 2019 John was in court because charges against him for trespassing had been dropped and he was seeking compensation. But he still wanted to have his say on the British legal system, accusing the judge of being an 'idiot' and a 'blackmailer'. Verdict? Innocent, although he was also warned in the summary that he must not tell judges they are 'blackmailing idiots'.

AND FINALLY...

If you're thinking to yourself, 'What did John do for a living before he found himself frequently in the courtroom?', and somehow you came up with the answer 'police officer', you would be right.

THE LAMBSHANK REDEMPTION

———

In 2016, the Institute of Directors, housed in a magnificent Georgian building in Pall Mall, London, UK, hosted a dining event with a difference. It began with a drinks reception at which the guests enjoyed prosecco produced by San Patrignano, an Italian organization that helps people with drug dependencies.

Meanwhile, a group of British ex-offenders representing a charity called The Clink worked in the kitchen to make the canapés. They also helped the front-of-house team. After dinner, The Clink's CEO, Chris Moore, spoke about giving inmates hospitality skills that would move them from time served to serving haute cuisine.

The charity runs restaurants at two prisons – Brixton and Styal – as well as a Clink Café in central Manchester. 'We're helping [the customers] to understand that the prison population is made up of a cross-section of society, just like you and me,' says Chris.

To visit one of The Clink's restaurants you have to go through much the same checks and security procedures as you would when visiting a prisoner. Not only have the restaurants consistently received rave reviews from food critics but those security checks also mean you'll never see a diner taking a picture of their food on their phone. And many would argue that that can only be a good thing.

AND FINALLY...

Jeff Henderson was arrested for dealing drugs in 1988, aged 24. He spent most of his ten-year sentence inside Terminal Island's Federal Correctional Institution in California, USA, and that is where he learned how to cook. In 2001, Jeff became the first African-American chef de cuisine at Caesars Palace, Las Vegas, and in 2020 he launched the Chef Jeff Project to help young disadvantaged people living in the Las Vegas community by offering professional training.

MY STORY

Cris Raducanu

Two weeks after Romania played Scotland in a rugby match at Murrayfield in 1989, reports emerged about a player who claimed political exile after escaping the watchful eye of the Romanian secret police. This is the story of what really happened and how Cris became an 'honorary Yorkshireman'.

❝ In the 1970s and early eighties, there was food and fuel in abundance in Romania. But also in the early eighties, [Romanian dictator] Nicolae Ceaușescu had this bright idea that he would pay off Romania's national debt by exporting everything the country produced. He achieved his dream by making everybody else's life a nightmare. There were queues for everything. People had to travel and wait for hours just to get a loaf of bread.

But one way for leaders to show how great communism was to the outside world was through performance in sports, and sport was huge in Romania. We finished second to the USA in the medals table at the 1984 Olympics. Yet it was also a closed society. You could only watch on TV what the government allowed you to watch.

Playing rugby allowed me to experience a different life, outside of Romania. I became our youngest international player when I was 16 and I was the youngest forward to play in the first World Cup in 1987.

I came from a privileged background. My dad was a senior figure in the military and my mother was the Romanian Royal Mail syndicate president. She had three secretaries in her office. But I could see what was happening in my own country and I thought, 'This is not for me, this is not what I want for my family'. When my daughter was born in 1989, me and my wife agreed that we wanted to give her a better way of life.

There wasn't a plan to defect, but I said it could happen in Edinburgh, although it was just talk. Then, on 9 December 1989 we lost 32–0 to Scotland. Actually, I had a good game!

We had the secret police monitoring our moves whenever we played abroad, but it was around 1 a.m. during an official post-match dinner at a hotel in Edinburgh that I spotted an opportunity, ran out of the hotel, took a right at the lights and saw a police car. Every time there is an international in Edinburgh it is pretty wild and the first thing the policeman asked me was 'Are you p*ssed?'

I was in my official Romanian blazer and tie and I said to the police officer, 'This is who I am'. They took me to the police station for a formal interview and then handed me over to the Scottish immigration office.

The Romanian revolution started a week later. Within three weeks Ceauşescu was gone. I have no idea what would have happened if I'd have stayed. You are not free to pursue your dreams in a dictatorship. Two weeks after I defected, I was on the front page of the *Edinburgh Evening News*, my picture alongside Nadia Comăneci (who won five Olympic gold medals in gymnastics) who had also fled from Romania.

While I was in Edinburgh, I was offered a labouring job by a former Scottish rugby international, Norrie Rowan. He's a lovely man and had a successful business as a property developer with Scottish teammate Sean Lineen. So, I worked on their construction site, and when I joined Norrie he owned the Tron Tavern.

It was while we were working on the tavern that they discovered all these tunnels under the pub that ran through the middle of Edinburgh city centre. Norrie decided to put a plaque there that read 'This is where Cris Raducanu escaped'. It's a nice story, but that's just a myth!

Leaving Romania was a chance we knew we had to take. It could have been years before I saw my wife and daughter again. But because of the revolution, we were reunited six months later. We eventually settled in Yorkshire and now run a property business. And I'm proud to call myself an honorary Yorkshireman. I was the first rugby player to represent Yorkshire that wasn't born in the county. They changed the rules to allow me to play. We also developed a community church in Farnley for Romanian people who had settled over here. Now we are very fortunate to have friends across different nationalities and communities.

Because of the help I got from people when I came here as a 20-year-old, I try to give back every day. **"**

BEYOND THE CALL OF (JURY) DUTY

———

J ury duty. Two words that can strike fear or excitement in the hearts of adults. Some relish the idea of striking a blow for justice, while others dread the thought of a long, drawn-out trial.

Anyone who has watched a US TV courtroom drama will be familiar with the process of 'voir dire', whereby jurors are asked about whether they can be fair and impartial. Attorney William Kelly told the *New York Daily Post*, 'I had a case once where the attorney on the other side asked, "Have you ever had experience with an attorney?" The woman answered, "You picked me up at a bar five years ago".'

In Clark County, Washington, USA, judges were asked about the worst excuses given by the public to get out of jury service. Judge Suzan Clark recalled one woman who said she couldn't do it because she needed to meditate for ten minutes every hour.

Another attorney, Steven Sladkus, said the most outlandish excuse he ever heard was somebody claiming that 'My planet does not believe in the jury system'.

In 2014, a jury summons addressed to IV Griner was sent from Cumberland County Courthouse in New Jersey, USA. When Barrett Griner IV picked up the letter his first thought was, 'Nobody in my house is named IV except the German Shepherd'. As a result of a computer error, his dog IV had been asked to do jury service. And no, she didn't turn up.

TOY STORY

On 1 April 2001, a branch of the Hooters restaurant chain in Panama City Beach, Florida, USA, ran a competition among its waitresses to see who could serve the most beer in a month. The winner would receive a brand-new Toyota. Or so they thought.

Jodee Berry finished top of the charts and eagerly anticipated receiving her prize, especially when she was led blindfolded into the restaurant's car park, only for the big reveal to show that she had won a toy Yoda: a doll version of the character from *Star Wars*.

What her bosses failed to anticipate was how the joke would backfire. Jodee not only quit her job but decided to sue their asses for 'breach of contract and fraudulent misrepresentation'. A year later, a court ruled in her favour and she received an undisclosed sum – although her lawyer said it was enough to buy that new Toyota, and probably another toy Yoda to go with it.

Philip White has a track record for taking out class actions against brands for false advertising, with mixed results. Most recently he filed a lawsuit against the makers of Texas Pete hot sauce because it is made in North Carolina, USA. The case was dismissed. One can only guess what White would make of living in the UK and discovering that Madrí lager, which is promoted as 'Madrid's modern lager', is made in Tadcaster, North Yorkshire. It is a triumph of marketing, or 'triunfo del marketing', as they say in Embajadores (and maybe Tadcaster).

THE RIGHT SIDE OF THE LAW

L awyers often get a bad rep and, at times, it is with some justification. When Darryl Cooke and Sarah Goulbourne founded the law firm Gunnercooke in the UK in 2010, they wanted to use their expertise to make a positive difference. They recognized that what large charities often have, but smaller ones lack, is the money to pay for professional help. It is one of the reasons why just 1 per cent of the UK's 165,000 charities account for 71 per cent of the sector's income.

The firm set out to level the playing field. Every one of their staff gives up their time to provide advice to small and medium-sized charities to accelerate growth, and reach a wider audience, as well as helping those who are struggling to stay afloat in the aftermath of COVID.

Darryl and Sarah also wanted to tackle another consequence of the pandemic – 45 per cent of people in the UK feel lonely, according to the Campaign to End Loneliness. The answer was to create a bookshop, café and events space inside a Grade II-listed building on King Street, Manchester, called the House of Books & Friends.

It opened in December 2022, with a mission to help rebuild communities – the proceeds are given to not-for-profit partners and charities that work to reduce social isolation. The House of Books & Friends has become so popular that it now hosts anything from 'meet the author' events to a 'children's story time' and even weddings.

LIES, DAMNED LIES AND CRIME STATISTICS

Japan has one of the lowest crime rates of any country in the world, but also the highest rate for convictions. The reasons for that are manifold, but often due to the length of time that somebody can be held in custody (23 days), which some have suggested leads to those arrested eventually confessing to crimes following prolonged interrogation.

Back in the early 1980s, a competition was held among policemen in Tokyo to see who could get the most convictions. It resulted in one petty criminal being arrested 108 times. The man later managed to get 71 of those arrests thrown out of court, despite confessing to each and every misdemeanour. He explained that he'd only done so because two officers had been trying to win the competition and had given him gifts, including rice, wine and cinema tickets, in return for those confessions. Justice was ultimately served, though, when he was acquitted, and the two policemen were arrested instead.

WHAT COULD POSSIBLY GO WRONG?

———

It was almost the perfect crime. In 2002, Chris Harn was a computer programmer working for Autotote, the company that processed over 60 per cent of bets staked at racecourses across the USA. He discovered that there were millions up for grabs in winning bets that had never been claimed.

So, Chris produced exact copies of those tickets and enlisted two friends, Derrick Davis and Glen DaSilva, to go to various tracks, claim other people's winnings, and split the proceeds, which ran into hundreds of thousands of dollars. Inevitably, the more bets they claimed, the higher the risk of eventually being caught out. So Chris then decided to go for one big payday. Having designed parts of the Autotote system, he realized he could game that system.

The Breeders' Cup is one of the biggest betting events of the year. One of the bets is called a Pick 6, in which you have to select the winners of six consecutive races. After four races, he knew there would be a half-hour window in which he could alter a bet.

Derrick staked six bets and Chris changed them to the known winners after the fourth race, while adding every runner in the fifth and sixth races, meaning they were guaranteed a cut of the $3.1 million jackpot. Chris assumed there would be other winners of the jackpot and that therefore nobody would notice the scam. The only thing that could go wrong, did go wrong.

The rank outsider won the last race at odds of 43–1 and suddenly Derrick found himself with the only jackpot-winning ticket. The Feds soon took an interest, with all three arrested and sent to prison a year later in what became known as the Fix Six scandal.

It was subsequently revealed that Autotote knew there was a fault but didn't want to spend the money trying to fix it.

THE MAN AND THE IRON BARS

The Brink's-Mat Robbery was dramatized in the 2023 BBC One series *The Gold*. Mick McAvoy was known as the mastermind behind a heist at London's Heathrow Airport that saw the robbers steal £26 million in gold, although the bullion was found by accident.

Mick's nephew John McAvoy maintained the family business by becoming a career criminal. He was arrested in 2005 for armed robbery and given a double life sentence. The turning point came when he was still in prison and made a phone call to his cousin, who told him that his [John's] best mate, Aaron Cloud, had died when his getaway car overturned after committing a robbery in the Netherlands.

John went to the prison gym, got on a rowing machine for the first time and became obsessed with rowing, to the point that he set a new world record for the most distance covered in 24 hours. He was mentored by prison officer Darren Davis and they've remained friends ever since. John was released in 2012, and now regularly competes in Iron Man contests.

In 2023, he launched the Alpine Run Project with the backing of Nike. John took 12 young people from disadvantaged backgrounds and trained them to compete in the Ultra-Trail du Mont-Blanc, the highest profile event in trail running.

AND FINALLY...

Georgia Durante was a New York model who, one evening, had her car flagged down because a man had been shot. What she didn't know was that the passengers worked for the Mafia. They were so impressed by her road skills that she became a getaway driver and regularly transported large bags of money to two men at JFK Airport who worked for the CIA but would launder that money on behalf of the Mob. Georgia then married a gangster but, fearing for her life, she fled New York and drove to Los Angeles, where she went on to put those driving skills to better use as a stunt driver in Hollywood movies.

HEADS I WIN, TAILS YOU LOSE

There are two things you can usually guarantee on any election day. One is people posting pictures online of dogs at polling stations and the other will be pictures of the candidates voting for themselves. However, when Damion Green stood for election to get a seat on the Rainier City Council in Washington, USA, he chose not to vote for himself. It took several weeks to count the ballots, and when they were finally totalled in December 2023, Damion had lost to Ryan Roth by just one vote.

Speaking to the local TV station, Damion said of his decision, 'I thought it was kind of narcissistic, so I didn't.' Ryan had also questioned whether he should do it, and was only talked into voting for himself by his wife. Had Damion voted it would have been a tie. Then, because there is no state law determining what happens in the event of a tie, the decision would have been settled by the toss of a coin – that was how an election was decided in 2015 just 8 miles [13 kilometres] away in Tenino. 'I would have called tails,' said Ryan.

IN GOOD SPIRITS...

A decade or so ago, hunting for artefacts with metal detectors was seen as something of an eccentric hobby. The wonderful BBC series *Detectorists*, which first aired in 2014, has helped to popularize the pastime significantly.

However, the most substantial find on English soil happened back in 2009, courtesy of a metal detector bought by Terry Herbert for just £2.50 at a car boot sale. What became known as the Staffordshire Hoard made him a millionaire; it was the largest collection of Anglo-Saxon gold and silver metalwork ever found, comprising over 4,000 items.

Terry later explained that plenty of detectorists had searched the same field, but failed to dig deeper. On this particular day, 5 July, Terry said to himself, 'Spirits of yesteryears, take me to where the gold appears'. And the spirits did their work.

Terry contacted Duncan Slark at the Birmingham Museum and recalled that 'When [Duncan] saw one box on the table, he just went "Wow". He said, "Is this it?" I told him there's another six boxes...'

According to law, Terry had to split the £3.2 million fund with landowner Fred Johnson. An event was held to mark the tenth anniversary of the discovery of the Staffordshire Hoard, but there was a significant no-show.

Terry refused to turn up. Before the find he and Fred had been friends, but they fell out, seemingly over the money, and have not spoken since.

BURIED TREASURE

—

Mike Spinelli is a writer and founder of the car-culture website Jalopnik. One day he was doing some random searches online and stumbled across an old story about a couple of kids who found a Ferrari Dino buried outside their house in West Athens, Los Angeles, USA.

For years, nobody knew exactly how it had got there. In 2012, Mike wrote a story about the incident, posted it on Jalopnik and then he got a call from Brad Howard, the man who now owns that very same Ferrari. The car was originally purchased in 1974 by

Rosendo Cruz, a plumber, who bought it as a birthday present for his wife. A week later he took her out to dinner at the Brown Derby, a Los Angeles dining institution. While they were perusing the menu, the car was being stolen for an insurance scam.

But instead of destroying the Dino, Cruz and his hired robbers decided they would keep it, hide it and collect it after the insurers had paid out. They never came back for their prize. Perhaps they forgot where they'd buried it.

Meanwhile, the car remained in remarkably good condition, despite being covered in earth, largely because of a drought in LA that lasted for two years, which prevented moisture from causing irreparable damage. Initially, detectives called to the scene feared they would find a body inside the car. Thankfully, they didn't.

Mike also discovered that the tale about the kids finding the car was a nice story for the press – detectives had been tipped off about the disappearing Dino by an informant.

One of the first things that Brad did once he'd purchased the Dino for $18,000 (around $65,000 in today's money) from a car dealer who had bought it in an insurance auction and restored it, was change the number plates. They now say 'DUGUP'.

AND FINALLY...

In possibly the worst attempt to pull off an insurance settlement, Carla Patterson and her son Ricky filed for a $500,000 pay-out from a Cracker Barrel restaurant in Virginia, USA, after claiming she had found a mouse in her soup. An investigation found that not only did the mouse not have any trace of the liquid in its lungs (for the record, it was vegetable soup), it also hadn't been cooked. The Pattersons were sentenced to one year each in prison for extortion.

A FORTUNE THROUGH GOING BUST

In the UK they're known as charity shops, but in America they're known as thrift stores, with the biggest chain being Goodwill. We use these shops knowing that the money we spend will go to good causes, but many customers also browse in the hope of snapping up a bargain.

In 2018, Laura Young bought a marble bust from a Goodwill store in Austin, Texas, for $34.99. Having been an antiques seller since 2011, she instinctively felt that it could be very old, possibly even dating back to Roman times. And she was right.

Laura got in contact with an expert from Sotheby's auction house and eventually received confirmation that the bust was 2,000 years old. It had gone missing from the Pompeiianum, a reconstructed villa in Aschaffenburg, Germany, inspired by the lost Roman city of Pompeii.

The villa had been bombed and abandoned during the Second World War. It remains a mystery how exactly the bust got into the USA and found its way to a Goodwill – there was no record of the donor. However, it was presumed to have been stolen by a US soldier from the Allied Forces. Laura was advised not to put it on the market because she could fall foul of the law and be arrested for selling stolen goods. So, it went on display instead.

Then, in 2022, Laura posted an update on Instagram to say the bust was on loan to the San Antonio Museum of Art. 'My nearly four-year relationship with a 2,000-year-old Roman portrait head owned by King Ludwig I of Bavaria and looted from the Nazis by the Allies/Americans in the Second World War has come to an end and I can FINALLY blab about him! If you know me personally you know I have a big mouth so this has been hard.'

CHAPTER EIGHT

STRON

TOGE

A MODEL COMMUNITY

———

'It's a small piece of England that will forever remain unspoilt. Neighbours all know each other, trains are never late, passers-by aren't in too much of a rush and the milkman still delivers gold top direct from the churn.'

So said one of the members of staff when Bekonscot, the world's oldest model village, celebrated its 80th birthday in 2009.

Back in 1927, Roland Callingham, a wealthy accountant by trade, wanted to build a swimming pool in the grounds of his house in Beaconsfield, about 20 miles [32 kilometres] north-west of central London, to entertain aristocrats, politicians, and movers and shakers. He had also built a huge model railway inside his house, but was told by his wife, 'Either the railway goes, or I do'.

So Roland took his hobby outside, built the world's largest model railway and then constructed a model village around the pool. Soon one village became five, before he added a model zoo, a harbour, a cricket pitch, a canal...

Every few years the village would be updated to move with the times, until a decision was taken in 1992 to go back in time. Now Bekonscot is permanently stuck in a 1930s time warp.

And, even though dozens of model villages across the UK have now closed down, Bekonscot's popularity endures. Over the years, more than £5.5 million worth of profits have been donated to local charities.

Perhaps part of its charm is that Bekonscot doesn't take itself too seriously. It is home to a dressmaker called Miss A. Stitch and a florist by the name of Dan D. Lyon, while the local greengrocer is known as Chris P. Lettis.

A LOCAL FUND FOR LOCAL PEOPLE

What would you do if you were given £1 million and told to spend it on making your community a better place to live? That is what happened in 2012 when the Big Local programme was launched to create what could be viewed as a social experiment on a massive scale.

Across England, 150 communities were each handed just over £1 million, with one stipulation: that the residents would decide how to spend it. The recipients mostly lived in communities that had among the highest levels of social deprivation in the country. Sceptics worried that residents would fritter the money away on frivolous projects and would lack the necessary organizational skills.

However, the programme ended up supporting projects that helped to restore confidence and pride in those communities.

These have included funding for what would become the Cheltenham Paint Festival, developing 40 dementia-friendly homes in Distington, Cumbria, a unique film project in Bromford, Birmingham (see next story), and a campaign started by a group of teenagers from Ewanrigg, Cumbria, which saw them invited to the House of Commons to discuss youth mental health.

Meanwhile, the residents of Lawrence Weston, near Bristol, formed a group called Ambition Community Energy and converted the original £1 million into £12 million worth of green energy investment. The area is now home to England's tallest wind turbine, providing a sustainable-energy blueprint for other communities.

ZOMBIES ARE PEOPLE TOO

———

There is a residential area in the UK that sits just within the boundary of Birmingham in the Midlands. It was once home to a steel mill, then it was given its own railway station, which provided the stop-off for Bromford Bridge Racecourse. Indeed, many of the roads in Bromford are either named after famous horses, like Arkle Croft, or racecourses, including Newmarket Way.

But in 1965 Bromford Bridge held its last race meeting and the land was turned into the Firs and Bromford housing estate. Historically it had been overlooked for investment, and it became what is often described as a 'left-behind' community, with all the negative impacts that come with that.

Because of that lack of investment, the Firs and Bromford neighbourhood became one of the communities chosen for the Big Local programme. So, what did they do with some of the money? They made a zombie movie. Of course.

The estate had a theatre group, who saw this as a unique opportunity to get people across Firs and Bromford working towards the common goal of making a film.

They partnered with Birmingham City University staff and students on a three-year project that included making three short films, including *Brombies*.

They also got to learn technical skills from experts in areas like video editing – skills that they otherwise wouldn't have been able to afford or learn at school.

Brombies itself was a statement on how people living on council estates are often perceived by members of the public and local government as outsiders that the rest of society wants to avoid.

As resident, and one-time Doctor Who impersonator, Phil Howkins explained, 'We get so much bad press. This is our way of getting everybody together, doing a fun project and getting the name of Firs and Bromford on the map.'

GOING UNDERGROUND

———

Coober Pedy (pronounced 'pee-dee') in South Australia has been likened to Bedrock, the home of the Flintstones, because half of its 2,500 population live underground in homes known as 'dugouts', built into sandstone. Coober Pedy is in the Australian desert, where temperatures can exceed 50°C (122°F), whereas these subterranean dwellings maintain a constant temperature of around 22°C (71°F). There are ventilation shafts above the surface, and the town generates most of its electricity from solar and wind power. There are no planning laws, so you can continue building underground, although that has, on occasion, resulted in somebody accidentally breaking through the rock into a neighbour's home.

The town is famous for its opal mines. People came here over 100 years ago in search of their fortune and began living underground in mineshafts. In 2003, local living legend John Dunstan, aka the Godfather of Coober Pedy, found the Virgin Rainbow Opal, which is worth over $1 million (AUS).

HIP-HOP FOR OAPS

———

'People do say to me, "hip-hop? Are you sure?" They think that I take fifty huge gangster rappers into a care home.'

Charlie Blair is the woman behind Blair Academy, a unique social enterprise in the UK. She is a breakdancer who studied Urban Practice at the University of East London but was more interested in getting other people to bust a move.

'Hip-hop comes from marginalisation,' she says. 'It comes from people that were oppressed, who didn't feel they had a voice in society and a lot of the groups that I work with are also marginalised.

'I started to ring around different places and said I wanted to try something new. A lot were taken aback. They thought I'd dialled the wrong number and said, "You do know we're a care home?" But a couple said, "Yeah, we'll give it a try".

'I've gone from being homeless to being self-employed to owning a business. I got to speak in Parliament about it and when BBC News covered us, we got bookings immediately. I also won a business competition at my old univeristy and received £6,000 in start-up money from NatWest [bank].'

To be absolutely clear, what Charlie does is go into care homes and encourage residents to be more active. It just so happens that the art form she uses to do that is hip-hop. 'Our main priorities are combating loneliness, strengthening communities, and bridging gaps, be it social or generational. So, we try to work with people who wouldn't otherwise do a hip-hop class.'

'The culture can be so beneficial when it preaches peace, love, unity and having fun. And we could certainly do with more of that!'

MY STORY
Xavier Wiggins BEM

Xavier is the co-founder of Dons Local Action Group (DLAG), a unique charity based in south London created by supporters of football club AFC Wimbledon when the UK went into lockdown in March 2020. He talks about the value of volunteering, being invited to the King's Coronation, and the future of sport and community action:

66 When, in 2002, AFC Wimbledon was founded by supporters (and I was one of them), our ultimate goal was to return home to Wimbledon, in our own stadium.

In 2019, we started work on constructing that stadium, but we were running out of money, needed £11 million and the banks weren't lending.

There was a fiery meeting in December 2019, where we were told we had 'to accept an offer of £7 million for 30 per cent of the club'.

The devil in the detail was that the fans would lose control of Wimbledon.

A couple of us stuck our hands up and said, 'We'll raise the money'. We hit the streets around the area and spoke to people. Lots of people. We said we wanted to build something really special, as a force for good in the local community.

We did it all through about 200 people on a WhatsApp group. We raised £5 million, the largest bond ever raised in English football, and Nick Robinson, founder of ASOS, put in £2.5 million. The rest we secured with a loan.

Then COVID happened. Anyone who knows me knows I'm not somebody who is going to sit around and do nothing. I sent a message to that WhatsApp group to see how we could help people in the community.

Five days later Dons Local Action Group (DLAG), which was co-founded between myself, Craig Wellstead, and Cormac van der Hoeven, had our first table outside a shop in the middle of Wimbledon, taking donations, which is still there to this day.

Soon we had three hubs and were outside 24 shops. We got a call from Siobhain McDonagh, the MP for Mitcham and Morden, who was talking about a hostel for homeless kids who had to homeschool but didn't have any laptops. So, we set up Keep Kids Connected, which is part of DLAG, to fix, repurpose and distribute old laptops.

Even now, on any given day, we'll have at least 100 volunteers out there, collecting and delivering food, furniture and laptops. We have to remember that somebody living in comfortable circumstances can lose their job, and then lose their house, so we try and look out for everyone.

And one of the most important things I've learned is how much the volunteers get from doing it. In some cases, it has helped them through difficult periods in their own lives.

Then, three years ago I discovered I'd been nominated and chosen for a British Empire Medal, which came as a total shock. Then, in 2023, I received a letter inviting me to the King's Coronation as one of 850 community and charity representatives. If somebody said I was going to the Abbey, I'd have thought we were playing Cambridge United away.

Then I checked the date and it clashed with Wimbledon playing away at Grimsby Town, so I wouldn't be able to go. I'm not into politics, I don't have a view on the royal family. I support my family and AFC Wimbledon. But the match got moved to a different date.

On the day of the Coronation, I must have looked an absolute mess when I arrived. I kept going up blind alleys. Security was tight. By the time I'd got there, I was perspiring and feeling somewhat scruffy. I then met this guy who was running a bit late like me. He was wearing about seventeen layers and not a hair out of place, not a bead of sweat on his brow. He was immaculate. He said he worked in fashion and lived in Milan, obviously.

I looked him up and realized he was Federico Marchetti, the chair of Fashion Task Force, a global sustainability organization, and he regularly speaks to the King. I had the Prime Minister a few seats away, various royals I didn't recognize...it was surreal.

And looking back, going to Grimsby would have been a ridiculous thing to do!

Going forwards, I want DLAG to be the start of something much bigger. I'm building an advisory board to ultimately create a membership body for sporting organizations, to harness their fanbases to build stronger communities. **"**

AN ENGLISHMAN'S CASTLE IS HIS HOME

———

E very working day, archaeologist Barry Mead would look out from his office and see the turrets of a pele tower, a small medieval castle in Cresswell, a village on the Northumbrian coast in the north-east of England. The Cresswell Pele (pronounced 'peel') Tower was on Historic England's 'Heritage at Risk' register and was slowly decaying. It was one of 175 such towers built across Northumbria during the late medieval and Tudor periods to protect the locals from the Scots. Until recently, only one was left open to the public.

Then the local holiday park said it wanted to hand over ownership of the tower to the parish council. Barry spotted an opportunity. He put forward a proposal to restore the tower and turn it into a local tourist attraction. Then he got people of all ages across the community involved, so that they would all have a stake in the future of the tower.

'We'll let children loose in the digging trenches – not many people do this – which means that they'll actually find things,' he told journalist Louise Tickle.

'Some kids from this area have been finding material which is 10,000 years old, from walking the ploughed fields. A headteacher nearby said that one of the pupils who wouldn't engage with school, who had taken part in some of our digs, just couldn't stop talking about it.'

Barry was named Community Archaeologist of the Year in 2019. The tower was then reopened in 2021, complete with a new roof, and it has become the focal point of Cresswell, and a source of great pride.

As Barry said in response to his earlier award, 'I love it. It's my passion, I'm digging, doing archaeology, yes, but importantly we're preserving our local heritage.'

AND FINALLY...

The Society of Thames Mudlarks and Antiquarians has been described as one of Britain's most exclusive communities. There are only 50 members, and it took ten years for one applicant to come off the waiting list. The term 'mudlarking' dates back to Victorian times, and was used to describe Londoners who scoured the muddy banks of the River Thames in search of treasure. The society's chairman, Tim Miller, told the *Times* newspaper that on one occasion a group of mudlarkers were rummaging around the foreshore of the Tower of London. They looked up to see soldiers pointing guns in their direction. 'They had permission to be there, but someone jumped to the wrong conclusion and thought they were terrorists,' he said.

THE NUTCRACKER? SWEET!

Steubenville, Ohio, USA, is typical of many towns that make up America's Rust Belt; towns that once thrived on producing cars, coal or, in Steubenville's case, steel.

The last steel mill closed in 2005, and some ten years later a community meeting was held to see what could be done to revive Steubenville. Jerry Barilla, who owned an appliance store, noted that in Cambridge, Ohio, they displayed life-size figures from Charles Dickens novels each Christmas and it not only gave the town some character, but also attracted visitors. Jerry suggested doing something similar but with nutcrackers (the German dolls, not the tools used to crack nuts). Mark Nelson, who ran a local gift-manufacturing store, said he would help and then Mark's family went into overdrive, making 37 giant nutcrackers.

Now there are more than 200 figures scattered throughout downtown Steubenville and its historic fort. Some are very traditional in appearance, but others depict famous fictional characters, such as Mary Poppins, Charlie Brown and Jack Frost. There is also one dedicated to singer and actor Dean Martin, a native of Steubenville, and another, Starman, was made in tribute to David Bowie after he passed away in 2016.

Jerry is now the mayor of Steubenville and he told the *Washington Post*, 'Parents and grandparents bring their kids to take memorable photos with the nutcrackers. It's just a delight.'

AND FINALLY...

When Larry Schmidt moved to the Glenview neighbourhood in Oakland, California, USA, his first experience of Halloween in his new home left him feeling that the spirit of the festival that he knew as a child was missing. For Larry, Halloween was about community, a chance to meet your neighbours or make new friends. Larry was a professional marionette puppeteer (the puppets with strings) and so he built a theatre in his driveway, wrote a script for a puppet show and named it *Driveway Follies*. The first *Follies* was staged in 2005 and Larry continued to pull the strings, along with a team of puppeteers, until he passed away in 2019. Larry's partner, Carl Linkhart, insisted that the show must go on and *Driveway Follies* continues to this day.

THIS LAND IS YOUR LAND

Lake Wakatipu has become one of the most popular tourist destinations in New Zealand. It has also become the country's equivalent of Billionaires' Row. All that money can give you the power and influence to do what you like.

On New Year's Eve 2022, ignoring objections from his neighbours, American billionaire Tony Malkin held a huge fireworks display, which got out of control and ended up torching half a hectare of land.

This makes the actions of farmers Dick and Jillian Jardine all the more laudable. In 2020, they gifted 900 hectares of land by the edge of Lake Wakatipu to the Queen Elizabeth II National Trust because 'it was the right thing to do', having turned down some serious offers for the land by developers.

'There's so much housing going…we want to be part of saving something,' said Jillian. On 1 July 2022, the land was officially handed over to the trust and it will continue to be a working farm, 100 years after it was first bought by Dick's grandfather. 'He would have loved it, he'd have been very proud,' Dick said.

FUNERAL FOR A STRANGER

Christina Martin is a stand-up comedian, author and prolific writer of letters to *Viz* magazine. She is also an Environmental Officer for Rother and Wealden District Councils in East Sussex, UK.

If somebody passes away with no next of kin, then their body becomes the responsibility of a council. In 2017, Christina was given a particularly challenging case when the body of a woman was found in the sea off the Sussex coast. The authorities did the usual checks and there was no record of her. Christina then had a month to see if she could track down the woman's identity before a funeral would be held.

An artist's impression was circulated – the woman was middle-aged, maybe around 40 years old – and yet still no one came forward. The idea that nobody would attend the funeral became a cause for Christina; she was determined that there would be a dignified send-off.

So, she took to social media and this was one of those moments where it was a force for good. Over 100 people turned up for somebody they didn't know. Many brought flowers to scatter over the coffin, some read eulogies and a wake was held in a local pub.

THE MOURNING AFTER

Through March and April 2010, a man turned up at a series of funerals in New Zealand to dish out his condolences and fill up Tupperware. He became known as 'the Grim Eater' and directors at a funeral parlour in Wellington issued a picture to warn mourners that if they saw a man brandishing plastic containers, he should be denied entry. Or words to that effect.

The Grim Eater was even pictured standing next to a hearse and giving a thumbs-up to the casket. The story became the subject of numerous columns, questioning whether his behaviour could, in any way, be condoned, especially as people said he was always courteous and respectful of the dead and no food ever went to waste. Then everyone moved on.

It turned out, however, that there was a bit more to this story. The man's name is Reece Tong, an artist who has been a regular at Pablos Art Studios, a community organization and gallery that supports mental wellbeing with free art materials, tuition and support. Pablos provides a safe environment for artists who have either been homeless or have mental health issues – Reece now lives in supported housing. His work has been displayed in galleries across different cities and countries.

BLOOMIN' MARVELLOUS

─────

If you had to find Aberfeldy on a map of the UK, your finger would probably hover over Wales, but the Aberfeldy in this story can be found in East London.

Over the years it had become a forgotten community. To compare Aberfeldy Street ten years ago to what it is now is a bit like that moment in the movie *The Wizard of Oz* when it goes from black and white to technicolour – from a grey, nondescript road to one where all the shop fronts are painted in different colours.

'Back then, there was nowhere to go in the evening,' says community leader Leila Lawal. 'The Aberfeldy Tavern used to be at the end of the road. It had been there since the 1950s but closed down in 2013. The developers put in a wine bar, closed that down, and then they put in apartments.'

Then local residents, supported by money from the National Lottery Community Fund, decided to create East London's first community boozer. The Tommy Flowers pub is on the site of what used to be a flower shop, but its name was actually chosen to honour one of Poplar's favourite sons.

Tommy was an engineer who worked with Alan Turing at Bletchley Park on the Enigma code-breaking machine that was crucial to the Allied Forces' war against Germany. He was later put in charge of the team that built Colossus, the first modern computer. A mural of Tommy graces the wall on the side of the pub, painted by Australian-born English artist Jimmy C, who was also responsible for the David Bowie mural in Brixton.

And just to add to the sense of togetherness, the interior was designed to look like somebody's living room, to make it as welcoming as possible.

AND FINALLY...

It was a long time coming, but in May 2023, the Travellers Rest pub in Skeeby, North Yorkshire, UK, finally re-opened. After closing in 2008, plans to convert it into a house stirred up local sentiment. So began a long but ultimately successful battle to bring it into community ownership. 'It is not for the faint-hearted. This has been a 15-year Herculean battle,' manager Carol Wilkinson told *ITV News*. 'Am I pleased we did it? Absolutely. Will it make a difference to the village? Absolutely.'

THE KIDS ARE ALRIGHT

———

For the best part of 40 years the Young Adults Centre (YAC) in Southall, Middlesex, UK, had been a place for people across different cultures to engage in activities, play sports or simply socialize. It was the focal point for young adults in that part of the world.

Then, in 2021, Ealing Council announced it would be shutting down the YAC, and the land would be sold to property developers. Step forward the Ealing Young Champions, a group of 14- to 19-year-olds who are passionately committed to improving their community.

They rallied local support, started a petition, got 1,500 signatures, held protests and eventually got to put their case to the council. Young Ealing Champion Lily Connolly-Woods, aged 18, presented the petition to councillors at a cabinet meeting and delivered a speech that was both measured and exceptionally well researched, making a compelling case for keeping the YAC. A year later, in September 2022, the council reversed its decision and said the centre would stay open. Better still, in April 2023 plans to invest £2.8 million in improving facilities at the YAC were revealed.

HELL IS OTHER PEOPLE...BUT NOT MOTORWAY TRAFFIC

In between the eastbound and westbound lanes of the M62 motorway, on the border of Lancashire and Yorkshire, UK, you will find a 15-acre farm and cottage.

Stott Hall Farm's history dates back to the eighteenth century but by the 1970s it looked as if its days were numbered, with the construction of the motorway that connects Liverpool to Yorkshire.

The farm acquired a cult status and a story was put about that the reason that it wasn't destroyed was because the owner, Ken Wild, refused to sell the land, deciding to stick it to the man. It's a myth that persists to this day.

In fact, there was a far more practical reason, which is that a geological fault below the farm made it impractical and too costly to bulldoze the area. Or, as current tenant Paul Thorpe explained, 'It was too wet and too steep...so they had to go around us'.

So what it is like to live on and run a 15-acre farm in the middle of what was described by the *Manchester Evening News* as the 'bleakest part of the motorway'? Surprisingly quiet. Well, indoors anyway, because all the windows are triple-glazed. Paul says you become accustomed to the noise of the cars. If anything, you're more likely to notice when traffic comes to a standstill because of a road accident.

At one time, Paul wondered if choosing to run a farm in the middle of a motorway would mean leading a forever single life, but he is now happily married to Jill. And together with their son John-William, they look after more than 900 ewes and 20 Angus cattle.

When she'd been asked to explain the benefits of living on Stott Hall Farm, Ken Wild's wife, Beth, had simply said, 'It's having no neighbours.'

CHAPTER NINE

WORLD

OF

SPORT

LOST IN TRANSLATION
(AND TRANSIT)

A report in the *Zambia Daily Mail*, dated 5 May 1990, exclaimed that 'Second Division British club side Leeds United arrived in Lusaka yesterday a slightly disgruntled lot after leaving their kit behind due to flight complications'.

'Leeds, who finished runners-up in the English Second Division League this year, arrived with twenty-two players and officials but their kit remained in Frankfurt, West Germany, because the flight they came on could not take the excess weight as it could not be allowed to refuel there.'

Leeds won the Second Division that year, but that's a minor oversight, especially when compared to the fact that United were nowhere near Zambia – the players were around 7,000 miles [11,000 kilometres] away celebrating their promotion to the First Division.

So who was at Lusaka Airport? Well, it was a group of students from Carnegie College, Leeds, being passed off as a professional football team.

Paul Jones, a member of the squad, said they couldn't understand why camera crews and photographers had turned up to greet them. Then they discovered they'd been booked into the best hotel in Lusaka. 'Nobody had stayed anywhere like it. We were a bunch of students being treated like royalty!', he recalls.

John Graham was a businessman who was in Lusaka and he was watching a TV news report about the team's arrival in disbelief.

'It was incredible. It wasn't made clear they weren't Leeds United,' he told the *Yorkshire Evening Post*. John added that team manager Colin Morris, 'was answering questions about promotion as if he was [Leeds manager] Howard Wilkinson'.

Colin was a football development officer for Leeds City Council and later explained that the tour was set up by the junior chamber of commerce in Zambia. He was contacted a year earlier in the hope of getting the real United to play, including Gordon Strachan, Lee Chapman and Chris Kamara.

Colin responded, saying there was no chance of that happening but that he could put together a team for a 'goodwill tour' on behalf of the city of Leeds. He also maintained that he was simply responding to questions about Leeds at the airport. As for the player who appeared in the *Zambia Daily Mail* above a caption saying 'Gordon Strachan', he just happened to have ginger hair.

Carnegie failed to win any of their three matches against Zambian club sides and word got around that a bunch of lads barely out of their teens and blessed with slightly above-average footballing ability might not be members of a squad that two years later would go on to win the First Division title, finishing ahead of Manchester United.

Carnegie beat a swift retreat out of the country following the final match to avoid an international incident. All sorts of wild stories circulated after they landed back in England, including rumours of a riot by fans when it became clear they had been conned, to a player being shot (not fatally) when his side only managed to draw 1–1 with the visitors from Leeds.

So why did a bunch of students get passed off as pros?

According to Paul Jones: 'Apparently for the tour to pay its way, or make a profit, the promoters advertised us as Leeds United', and the kit getting 'lost in transit' served to maintain the ridiculousness of the ruse.

Creighton University's American football team from Nebraska, USA, played its last game in 1942. Some 40 years later the university paper ran a spoof story about Creighton going unbeaten through the season. Even though every match report featured a disclaimer that 'the following story is entirely fictional', the media thought it was true to the point where CBS turned up with a news crew and had to film footage of a fake team.

THE RACE OF THEIR LIVES PART I

U S marathon runner Frank Shorter was well clear of the field when he entered the stadium for the men's marathon at the 1972 Olympic Games in Munich.

So imagine how he felt when he saw another runner who was well clear of him. Norbert Sudhaus was a 17-year-old West German student who had ripped the number '72' off a poster advertising the Olympics, put it on his running shirt, jumped on the back of a golf cart being driven by one of his friends who was working inside the Olympiastadion, and then suddenly appeared on the track, in front of thousands of people, many of whom were oblivious to the fact that he had blagged his way into race.

Soon after, Frank entered the stadium bemused by the fact that he could hear some booing because sections of the crowd thought he was the closest threat to Sudhaus taking the gold medal for Germany. Then he heard an American shout from the stands, 'Don't worry, Frank!'

Frank had little clue about what was going on in front of him until he crossed the finish line and was immediately asked, 'What do you think of that guy?' Frank realized what had happened. Meanwhile, Norbert ran past officials, through a tunnel and straight back out of the Olympiastadion.

Some people were indignant that Norbert had stolen the winner's moment of glory, but as Frank later said, 'In a way, people perhaps remember the race more because of that. And I was much less upset than the people who saw it.'

Indeed, the commentators for ABC Sports were apoplectic. Erich Segal shouted into his mic, 'That is an imposter. Get him off the track!' before screaming, 'It's a fake, Frank!', as if the runner could hear him. Obviously, he couldn't.

Co-commentator Jim McKay interjected, 'It's like the time when an American in 1904 hitched a ride on an automobile and tried to cheat and win the marathon'. Well, funny you should say that, Jim, because...

THE RACE OF THEIR LIVES PART II

———

The Olympic Games always produce incredible stories, but there has never been an event quite like the 1904 marathon held in St Louis, USA. Here are the edited highlights, one for each mile of the race...

1. Thirty-two runners started the race; only 14 finished.
2. The field included Thomas Hicks, who was born in Birmingham, UK, but raced for the USA and was a clown by trade.

3. The man who designed the course, James E. Sullivan, was a profoundly racist and misogynistic man who barred US women from competing in the 1912 Olympics.

4. Sullivan also believed drinking or eating during a race was bad for the runners...

5. ...which explains why there were only two water stops on the route, and the second one was actually a water well.

6. The runners competed on a day that reached 32°C (90°F).

7. The field featured Frank Pierce, the first Native American to compete at the Olympic Games...

8. ...and also included Len Taunyane and Jan Mashiani, the first two black South African Olympians.

9. Len went a mile off course after being chased by wild dogs but still managed to finish ninth.

10. They would also become the last black athletes to represent South Africa until 1990, when apartheid had been abolished.

11. Cuban runner Félix Carvajal turned up penniless after losing his money gambling and was wearing trousers that had to be cut down before the race started.

12. During the race, Félix chatted with spectators.

13. He later grabbed an apple from an orchard to satisfy his hunger, but the apple was rotten and gave him stomach cramps.

14. He took a nap to help ease his pain, woke up and ran on to finish fourth.

15. American William Garcia was hospitalized after inhaling dust from the track that ripped his stomach lining.

16. Fellow American Fred Lorz broke down with cramp after 9 miles [14 kilometres]. He then got a lift in a car that took him 11 miles [18 kilometres], completed the course on foot, and was crowned the winner until he got rumbled, claimed it was a joke, and received a lifetime ban from competing. The ban was later rescinded and he went on to win the 1905 Boston Marathon.

17. Some reports say Fred was known as a prankster. Whether he would have confessed of his own accord, we'll never know.

18. Thomas Hicks's coaches gave him a combination of egg whites and strychnine sulphate.

19. Strychnine is a poison often used to kill rats, albeit using much higher quantities.

20. Thomas was later given more strychnine with a swig of brandy to wash it down, to help him through the last mile.

21. At that point, he started hallucinating and thought there were still 20 miles [32 kilometres] to go.

22. He became the Olympic champion with the slowest winning time ever recorded, clocking in at 3 hours and 28 minutes.

23. That's almost 30 minutes slower than any other Men's Olympic marathon, even though it was run over 24.85 miles [40 kilometres] instead of the standard 26.2 miles [42.195 kilometres].

24. Frenchman Arthur Corey finished second but is listed in the records as American because he didn't have any documentation.

AND FINALLY...

The most raucous reception for any runner who competed in the Women's Marathon at the 1984 Olympics in Los Angeles, USA, was reserved for Gabriela Andersen-Schiess who finished 37th. Gabriela was in all sorts of agony as she entered the stadium for the final lap, but refused to let any officials touch her as that would have meant being disqualified. She completed that final lap in 5 minutes and 44 seconds to a standing ovation.

THE MOTHERS OF RUGBY

Against all odds, Wales hosted the first Women's Rugby World Cup in 1991. The International Rugby Board refused to recognize it as an official event, the French pulled out at the last minute and the USSR planned to pay their way by smuggling in vodka, caviar and Russian dolls and selling them on the streets of Cardiff. While the contraband was confiscated by the South Wales Police, nobody was arrested because they couldn't crack the language barrier.

USA won the final, creating an almighty upset by beating England 19–6, with a squad that included Candi Orsini, a Hollywood stuntwoman. 'Learning how to relax your body when you get hit [in rugby] comes in handy when you flop over the hood of a car,' she said.

The team also featured Tara Flanagan and Tam Breckenridge, aka the 'locks from hell'. 'It was a joke,' explained Tara. 'We're very nice people, but we want to be your worst nightmare on the rugby field. So, the "locks from hell" just kinda stuck.'

After seeing his team beat New Zealand in the semis, US coach Kevin O'Brien bumped into one of England's coaches in the toilets. 'The thing is, I'm from Cardiff, I've got a Welsh accent and he didn't know who I was or that I was representing the USA,' said Kevin.

'He said to me, "Yeah, it was a good game and, you know, it'll be tough on Sunday but we'll have it." The English coach didn't think the Americans would be tactically and mentally strong enough to win.' Kevin left without saying another word.

'Back then, USA Rugby really wanted nothing to do with us or the tournament, but they did send me four or five ties to give to the opposition after the game. We beat England 19–6. There was an event following the final, we made a little speech and then I came face-to-face with that coach. As I handed him his tie, he gave me this look, like, "Just don't do it, don't say an effing word!"'

That first World Cup was as much about freedom of expression as it was about playing the game.

'Across so many other sports, the rules were different for women,' explained Kevin. 'Anything that included physical involvement was frowned upon. But rugby was a chance for everybody, no matter who they were, to play the way the men did. One of the things I'm most proud of was being involved in the early stages of the women's game in America.'

'I like to say, and I don't know if it's exaggerating, but rugby has saved my life in a way because people are there to help you.' So said Mui Thomas, now based in Hong Kong, in an interview with Alex Mead of the *Rugby Journal* in 2021.

Mui was born with harlequin ichthyosis, an extremely rare condition that means her skin grows 14 times faster than average, and she has exceptionally brittle bones. She loved rugby, but her skin condition meant that she was unable to play professionally, so she became a referee instead. 'I love to be involved so I'll ref as long as they let me be there,' adding that, 'I go out each day and I have the same struggles as most people: I forget my keys, my wallet, my brain sometimes. I'm like everybody else, I live my life the way I can, and if people find that inspirational, me just living my life, then that's great.'

RISK JOCKEY

O ne of the Grand National's most celebrated riders never got close to winning the race, and either broke or fractured 107 bones in seven attempts at trying to complete the course.

Spanish aristocrat Beltrán Alfonso Osorio y Díez de Rivera, aka the 18th Duke of Alburquerque, became known in the UK as the Iron Duke.

His final ride at Aintree in 1976 left him in a coma for two days. Undaunted by this brush with mortality, he planned to come back the following year, only to have his jockey's licence in the UK revoked for his own safety, a decision that prompted his friend and legendary trainer Fred Winter to say, 'I am both saddened and relieved'.

Instead, the Duke had to watch the race from the stands and he described the experience as 'the saddest moment in my life'.

He believed his popularity was explained by being something of a curiosity, 'like an Englishman becoming a bullfighter', he said.

His obsession with Aintree began as an eight-year-old, when he saw a newsreel of the race. The Duke's first ride on Merseyside came in 1952, which also led to his first, but far from last, visit to Walton Hospital after suffering from concussion and a cracked vertebra.

Two weeks before the 1974 race, the Duke had 16 screws removed from his leg. Then, further disaster struck seven days ahead of the Grand National, when he broke his collarbone following a fall at Newbury.

He faked his way through a medical to ensure he could still ride at Aintree and remarkably still finished eighth on Nereo, in a race won by Red Rum. When asked to explain why he continued to put his neck, and pretty much everything else, on the line for the sake of a horse race, the Duke simply replied, 'Without risk, there is no emotion'.

AND FINALLY...

The race that first sparked the Duke's fascination with the National was Tipperary Tim's win in 1928. A pile-up at Canal Turn took out many runners, and by the time they'd reached the penultimate fence, only three horses were left in the race. Great Span was in the lead but his rider's saddle slipped. Then Billy Barton fell. Although his jockey remounted, he'd lost all momentum, allowing Tipperary Tim to win at odds of 100–1.

MY STORY

Dr Ayaz Bhuta MBE

Ayaz was a member of the Great Britain Wheelchair Rugby (GBWR) team that won gold at the Tokyo Olympics in 2020. He overcame multiple operations, self-doubt and prejudice to make Team GB. Since retiring from wheelchair rugby in 2022 he has used his achievements to inspire other disabled kids to take up sport...

❝ The moment I received my gold medal, I was thinking about my mum who passed away in 2010. She never got to see me in this sporting environment, playing wheelchair rugby. She never got to see me represent Great Britain. It happened just as I started on this journey. Then I felt this overwhelming sense of spirituality.

Muslims believe in patience and trusting in God's plan. Before sunrise, every morning I always used to make a duʿāʾ, which is a prayer, and I would say 'If a medal is good for me, then let it happen. And if it's not good for me then I will understand.'

I was born with Roberts syndrome, a rare condition which affects growth. I was in and out of hospital for fourteen years. A child once asked me, 'How did that feel?' All the way through childhood I had major operations on my limbs, my eyes, my legs, you name it. I remember that I used to bawl my eyes out when they took me to the operating theatre. Eventually, I got used to that. But I was also determined and strong-willed.

When I went back to school, I was always made to feel wanted or special. That also helped me get through it. But I struggled to make friends at college; I felt conscious about my identity. I put on weight, I lost my confidence in talking to people, I retreated into my shell.

Then a teacher suggested trying wheelchair basketball. I joined Bury Blue Devils. All the weight dropped off, and my confidence came back.

But I just kept ramming into opponents, which you're not allowed to do in basketball. I was getting squared up to by people who were twice my size and weight. Then rugby came calling and they said, 'You can ram into chairs and do it legally!'

I seemed to have a natural ability [for wheelchair rugby], to take on people, learn how to take hits and how to position my chair, so I don't get hit on the sweet spot and fall out. After we finished fourth [in the 2016 Olympics] we said, 'What do we want to change about GBWR?'

Firstly, we wanted to create our own legacy. We wanted to be the first GB team and the first European team to win a medal. We were really well prepared [for Tokyo] and I think that showed. Of course, there was pressure, but we came home with gold.

When I returned home to Bolton, there was a surprise street party held in my honour. There was family, childhood friends, people from the community…Everyone was so kind, but that's the power of a gold medal, isn't it? I even get free chicken and chips from the local takeaway. I'm living the dream!

I believe that the gold medal has a higher purpose. I see it as a gift and how can I use this gift to make the world a better place for others? In South Asian culture, disability is treated as a taboo subject. I remember my parents getting treated a bit differently by other relatives; there would be nasty comments at weddings, 'Your kid is not normal like my kids'. So, that's why I visit faith schools and do community work, to try to change perceptions in any way that I can.

Parents worry about their children prospering in life. How are they going to get a job, meet a partner, get married, how will they fit into their community? But often they're not as focused on what that child needs at that moment in time, and I've spoken to parents about how sport has had such a positive impact on my independence and confidence.

Anytime I see somebody with a child who has a disability, I make an effort to speak to them. Or I talk to teachers about the opportunities that are out there and hopefully I can open a few doors. Obviously we have to be careful because not everybody can be a Paralympian. But, you know, if I can get one kid to join a team, take up a sport, then that's the gift of winning a gold medal. **"**

MATCHES TO ASHES

P elé famously called football 'the beautiful game'. When Paul Gascoigne was reduced to tears after England lost in the 1990 FIFA World Cup semi-final to Germany on penalties, it became known as 'the crying game'. Meanwhile, Ajax, the most successful club in the Netherlands, knows all there is to know about 'the dying game'. A common final wish of football fans is to have their ashes scattered across the ground of the team they supported. But many clubs simply don't permit it. At least not officially.

In 1996, Ajax demolished the De Meer Stadion, which had been the club's home since 1933, to make way for the Amsterdam (now Johan Cruijff) Arena, at which point the club became part of an unlikely collaboration. A huge patch of turf from the old pitch was transported, along with the home team's dugout, to Herdenkingspark Westgaarde, a memorial park and crematorium on the outskirts of Amsterdam, to create the Ajax Memorial Field.

To this day, the relatives and friends of late Ajax fans can toss their ashes over the turf before having a moment of quiet reflection in the same dugout that was once graced by Cruijff, Marco van Basten and Rinus Michels, the legendary coach who invented the concept of Total Football.

AND FINALLY...

When, in 2023, Napoli became Italian football champions for the first time in 33 years, the supporters staged a mock funeral for other teams in Serie A. They even created a makeshift cemetery, with a coffin in the centre surrounded by 19 crosses, each one featuring the badge of a different Serie A team.

DOUBLE AMPUTEE, ZERO HANDICAP

B ob MacDermott from Saskatchewan, Canada, was a farmer and a half-decent amateur golfer. On 23 August 1987, Bob had two choices: go and play in his first tournament or do some work on the farm ahead of the harvest season. The decision to do farm work changed his life. Bob was driving a tractor-powered cultivator when the cultivator's shovel knocked into an electricity pylon, which broke, fell and hit the tractor.

Even though Bob was quick enough to move away from the equipment, he was still close enough for 14,000 volts to shoot through his body. And Bob's day was about to get a whole lot worse.

The ambulance taking him to the hospital blew two tyres while travelling at 85 miles [136 kilometres] per hour. The vehicle flipped and Bob was catapulted out of the back, into a field where dirt and stubble got into his wounds.

Not even nine skin grafts could prevent gangrene from setting into his arm, which, along with his left leg, had to be amputated, otherwise Bob would have died. Having survived, he seriously contemplated whether life was worth living.

Meanwhile, his wife was thinking, 'How will he play golf?' hoping that the sport might help Bob to focus on his rehabilitation. Her question was answered when he returned to the golf course a year later, with the aid of prosthetics.

'The first time I tried to hit some golf balls it hurt real bad. I almost cried,' Bob recalled. He shot 89 over nine holes, but the fact that he could simply strike a ball again was like getting a hole-in-one, and he says that golf saved his life.

In 2003, Bob shot 65 over 18 holes on his way to winning a tournament at the Belvedere Golf & Country Club in Alberta, Canada. He went on to become one of the world's leading amputee golfers. Or, as Bob would say: 'No arm, no leg, no problem.'

AND FINALLY...

Nullarbor Links in Australia is known as the 'world's longest golf course'. When they say long, it takes around five days to complete and measures 850 miles (or 1,365 kilometres) in distance, which is roughly as long as Manchester to Zurich. The holes are located in different towns or roadhouses along the Eyre Highway and the course was invented to give truckers something to do on such a long stretch of road. Author Oliver Horovitz played Nullarbor Links in 2017. 'We spot kangaroos and wombats and stop to peek inside secret caves. We try buffalo kebab (not bad),' he wrote. 'This is the great Australian adventure, with a golfing twist – and most other Australians have never experienced it.'

PUB FOOTBALL TEAM

———

Soon after Jahn-Eric Birkeland and his wife moved into their new home in Lyngdal, a village on the south coast of Norway, she said he could do whatever he liked with their vast basement. What she didn't anticipate is that he would convert the space into a boozer devoted to football team Manchester United, with enough room to seat 50 fans along with a very, very large screen.

The Little Old Trafford Pub cost around £50,000 to construct when it was built in 2002. Since taking first orders, it has become home to an impressive array of memorabilia, and Jahn-Eric has since added a 'mini-megastore' selling United merchandise.

Such is its fame that United legends have visited, including Eric Cantona in 2019. Over the past decade, the regulars have had to endure United going from the best team in the world to utter mediocrity. Yet, unlike the real Old Trafford, the roof never leaks, it's not prone to infestations of mice, and it won't take around seven hours to get back to Lyngdal after the match has finished and you've just been humiliated by Bournemouth.

———

AND FINALLY...

The bottom of the Blue Lake in Imotski, Croatia, is home to a unique football match between two local teams known as Werewolves and Elves. It only ever takes place if the lake completely dries out in the summer, which has happened ten times since 1943. The centre circle is marked out like the Mercedes-Benz symbol. This part of Croatia is home to more models of this luxury car per head than anywhere else in the world, many of which date back to the 1960s, when villagers went to work in Germany and often come back with a Merc as a sign of success.

GLADIATORS THROWN TO THE LIONS

———

The Dorchester Gladiators 3rd XV tour of Romania in 2000 is a worthy contender for the greatest trip ever undertaken by an amateur rugby club. A spectacular cock-up saw a motley crew of over-40s mistaken for a professional team. The story made the front page of the *Daily Telegraph* and led to an appearance on *This Morning with Richard and Judy*.

As club chairman Tony Foot explained, 'One of our touring party was a Royal Marine. He got in touch with a chap in Romania who said "Oh, you must come over here and visit us." So he replied and said "Yes, we've got a touring team, we're called the Gladiators..."'.

One of the organizers, who was also affiliated with the British Embassy, heard the name Gladiators and presumably associated them with professional teams like the Leicester Tigers and Sale Sharks. Suddenly, and unknowingly, the Gladiators had been matched up against Steaua Bucharest, Romania's most successful rugby team, who had played in the European Challenge Cup the previous year and had a squad packed with international players.

'When we arrived at the airport, we were met by one of [Steaua's] representatives who came in quite a swish coach with a sign saying "Dorchester Gladiators" in the window,' recalled Mark Andrews, who played on that tour. 'We thought, "Well this is very nice, this just must be how it is!" But then after we'd all got on the coach, the representative said, "Do you want to go to train at the stadium this evening?" At first, we looked at each other and thought "Train Stadium? Is that the name of a bar?" The penny was starting to drop that this wasn't going to be what we'd expected but we said "No".'

'We got talking to this very large man in an actual bar who said, "What are you doing in Romania?" We said, "We've come over to play a game of rugby tomorrow." "Ah, so you're the Gladiators!" he replied. "I'm playing against you at prop." So we thought, "if they're all this big, then we're in a bother". He explained he played for Steaua Bucharest but we still thought "Well we must be playing their second or third team".'

'We went to bed at around 5 a.m., for an 11 a.m. kick-off. When we arrived at the stadium there were cameras everywhere and the TV crews were set up. People were queueing up to get into the ground. Even then we were still of the view that, "Well, there must be a bigger game on this afternoon". We walked into the stadium and it dawned on us that we *are* the big game.'

A few of the Dorchester players sparked up cigarettes to prove they were really just a bunch of lads on a jolly in Bucharest. 'They seemed to think we had something up our sleeve,' explained Mark. 'We didn't.'

Losing 61–17 was a respectable result against players half their age and twice their ability. Soon the story got back home to the UK and the Gladiators were front-page news, before getting invited on to UK TV show *This Morning*.

One of the players took the mickey out of presenter Richard Madeley, who had recently been convicted for shoplifting. Richard didn't see the funny side.

'For a week it was the gift that kept on giving,' said Mark. 'It was our 15 minutes of fame.'

In one of sport's more extraordinary examples of mistaken identity, English Football League club Sunderland signed Honduran striker Milton Núñez from Greek club PAOK Thessaloniki for £1.6 million in 2000. Núñez only started one match for the club, who were in the Premiership back then. His limited game time could be explained by the fact they'd signed the wrong player and thought they were getting Milton's teammate Adolfo Valencia. Years later, Núñez added a further element of ridiculousness, saying that Sunderland had been looking at two PAOK players, Adolfo and Eduardo Bennett, who were both just under 6 feet [1.8 metres] tall and ended up with Núñez who is just 5 feet 5 inches [1.65 metres] tall.

HOLD MY BEER

Michael Lewis gave up playing American football in high school when he became a father and had to provide for his family. He became a delivery driver for Budweiser – the depot was just a short walk away from the Superdome, home of the New Orleans Saints. But he never turned his back on the game; instead he played for a series of semi-pro teams and slowly but surely moved up the leagues.

He did enough to earn a try-out for the Philadelphia Eagles but was released halfway through training camp. So, it was back to the day job. But his time at the Eagles was enough to spark interest from the Saints. He joined their practice team and excelled as a return specialist – the guy who receives the ball from a kick-off or a punt. In 2000, he started his rookie season for the Saints aged 30 and became the top return specialist in the NFL. Aged 35 he set a new record for punt and kick return yards in a season. Soon after, an injury brought Michael's career to an end. But, what a career.

AND FINALLY...

Among the many myths attached to the Super Bowl is that, in 1984, so many people went to the toilet at half-time that it caused a water main to burst in Salt Lake City. That said, the annual peak water flow will often happen during the half-time break, so systems are kept well prepared for such an amazing example of synchronization.

IN FOR A PENNY, IN FOR A FARTHING

The year 2023 marked the return of a bike event like no other in the UK. The Great Knutsford Race is only open to cyclists competing on a Penny Farthing, aka the bike with a big wheel and a tiny wheel, which got its name from the largest and smallest British coins in existence at the time when it first went on sale in 1870.

For 15 years it was the only bike that Brits could buy until a more conventional one was invented, virtually wiping out sales overnight. Yet, to this day, you can still find Penny Farthing clubs around the world.

The Great Knutsford Race was first held in 1980. There were only meant to be two competitors but quickly it mushroomed to 72.

Races have since been staged every ten years, but the 2020 event had to be postponed because of the COVID-19 pandemic, and it eventually happened three years later, with 113 men and women taking part, including Neil Laughton (see page 196). The winners are those who complete the highest number of circuits around a 900-metre [980-yard] course that snakes around the centre of Knutsford, a village in Cheshire. And this on a bike that is hard enough to navigate even before you learn that it has no brakes and no gears.

AND FINALLY...

For hardcore riders, the competition of choice is Sweden3Days – the Penny Farthing world's answer to the Tour de France. The first Sweden3Days was held in 2021. It was also the first Penny Farthing race staged in the country for over 100 years. Riders compete in four events over three days, including the finale, which is a two-hour endurance race. In the words of the organizers, 'These are men and women who fear nothing, not even coming last.' The crazy fools.

FANKNAPPED

———

W hen 50 football fans from Fulham boarded an Angel Motors coach on 14 January 1997, they assumed it would be taking them from south-west London, UK, to see their team play away at Colchester, Essex. But as the coach headed out of the capital, along the M11 motorway, it soon became apparent they weren't going to their intended destination.

When they told the driver he'd missed the turning for Colchester, he informed them that his instructions were to go to Cambridge, some 50 miles [80 kilometres] away, and he stubbornly refused to change course, despite the pleas from his passengers. Instead of watching the game, the supporters were held captive and received an impromptu tour of the university town.

Fulham fan Ian Bishop said: 'We explained he was going the wrong way, but he was having none of it. We spent six hours on that bloody coach and never got close to the ground. It was like being kidnapped.' Angel Motors received the red card and their services were no longer required by Fulham. Meanwhile, at least those supporters had a memorable story to recount, whereas the ones who made it to Colchester saw Fulham lose 2–1.

AND FINALLY...

When the club's former owners wanted to bulldoze Fulham's home at Craven Cottage and build luxury apartments, lifelong supporter Dennis Bailey stood up to the owners and successfully applied for the Riverside Stand, the Cottage and the turnstiles to be granted Listed status. Through his actions and those of fans who successfully ran a campaign to stop the development, this unique and much-loved stadium was saved.

CHAPTER TEN

WE COU

BE

LD
HEROES

THE MEN WHO SAVED THE WORLD

If you're not familiar with the name Stanislav Petrov, then you should be. On 26 September 1983, he saved the world.

Stanislav was a lieutenant colonel in the Soviet Air Defence Forces. On that day he received a message that five missiles launched by America were heading towards the Soviet Union. Standard procedure would have been to inform his superiors, who would then have launched a counterattack.

Stanislav and his colleagues believed (rightly) that the message was a fault in the missile tracking system and therefore did not report it. As a result, nuclear war was averted. Amazingly, his reward for taking decisive action was to be demoted, because he had failed to acknowledge the chain of command and taken it upon himself to decide that it was a false alarm.

It was 15 years before Stanislav's actions became public knowledge and his deed was acknowledged with a series of commendations and medals. In 2014, a documentary about him was released, titled *The Man Who Saved the World*.

Stanislav was always self-deprecating. He never sought publicity or attention for what he had done, and once said, 'All that happened didn't matter to me – it was my job. I was simply doing my job, and I was the right person at the right time, that's all.'

While Stanislav's story gained a wider audience over the years, there was also another man who prevented the world as we know it from being destroyed by a nuclear conflict. His name was Vasili Arkhipov, a Soviet naval officer on *B-59*, a nuclear submarine stationed near Cuba during the missile crisis of 1962.

At the time, the US government had made it clear that they would launch 'signalling depth charges' at any Soviet submarines found in waters around Cuba. A signalling depth charge was a missile that would serve as a warning to a submarine that it should come to the surface to be identified. However, *B-59* had been out of contact with radio traffic for several days because it was too far below the surface.

When the crew became aware of the depth charges, two of the most senior officers on board believed a nuclear conflict was underway, and they were ready to unleash a torpedo with a third of the power of the Hiroshima bomb.

Protocol required all three senior officers to agree to launch a warhead. Vasili objected and persuaded the captain that they should come to the surface and seek instructions from Moscow, thus preventing what would have almost certainly been the start of a third world war. Yet he never lived to see his story told to anyone outside Russia. According to the US National Security Archive, 'The submarine commanders tried to suppress the story of the incident on B-59 for almost 40 years.'

Vasili died in 1998, and 19 years later he was posthumously given the Future of Life Award, which 'recognises exceptional measures, often performed despite personal risk and without obvious reward, to safeguard the collective future of humanity'.

IN YOUR HONOUR

———

On any given weekday, thousands upon thousands of people will walk, cycle or drive along City Road, right in the heart of

London. On one stretch of that road there's a Sainsbury's Local, a Pret A Manger, a Tesco Express, another Pret...

But directly opposite the Tesco Express is the exterior of a small castle and virtually everyone who passes it will have little or no idea of its purpose or what goes on behind it.

The castle provides a striking facade to the Honourable Artillery Company (HAC), the oldest regiment in the British Army, founded in 1537 by Henry VIII and second only to the Swiss Guard, which protects the Pope, as the world's oldest military unit.

The five-acre site includes the immaculate lawns of the Artillery Ground. In 2016, those lawns hosted Queen Elizabeth II to mark her 64 years as Captain-General of the HAC and to unveil a bronze bust in her honour.

But it is the events of 7 July 2005 that will be forever etched in the memories of everyone who was at HAC on that day.

Given its location, the size of those lawns – and because of its status as a functioning military site that could immediately go into lockdown, with the space to accommodate medics, forensic teams and government officials – HAC was the logical and practical choice for a makeshift mortuary and forensics centre in the wake of the 7/7 bombings, which killed 52 people.

'All of sudden, the whole site was being requisitioned and all the forensic evidence was also stored here,' explained Major Charles Marment, who became an HAC Trustee but in 2005 was a serving army reservist.

'I always remember meeting the guy who installed the generator, and he said it would have powered Salisbury [which has a population of 45,000],' Charles added.

The Army then went into action. 'And that's what the Army does really well,' he explained. 'It arrives in a part of the world where everything's broken. Then, you know, suddenly someone finds a brush, someone knows how to make a cup of tea, someone's put up a tent, it springs from there and that's what we did.

'I got the Salvation Army involved, and they were just brilliant because nothing will faze them. When they turned up it was chaotic. They set up soup kitchens and served all-day breakfasts. It was just a massive team effort by a very resilient group of Londoners.'

MY STORY
Professor Andrew Deaner

On 16 March 2012, Andrew was a spectator sitting in the stands watching his team, Tottenham Hotspur, taking on Bolton Wanderers at Tottenham's old ground, White Hart Lane. After 43 minutes of the first half, Bolton footballer Fabrice Muamba collapsed and went into cardiac arrest. Andrew became a household name overnight as he helped save Fabrice's life. He speaks about the impact of that event and how it subsequently saved countless other lives:

❝ It was obvious how serious it was right from the start. I wouldn't have thought about going onto the pitch otherwise, because suddenly you had two doctors tending to a Premiership player in cardiac arrest in front of 36,000 people, and then some bloke in a cycling jacket appears and says, 'I'm a cardiologist'. Those doctors must have thought, 'What on earth?'

If you see the footage, I didn't really do anything on the pitch. It was when another cardiologist, Dr John Hogan, said to one of those doctors that he knew me, then they started taking more notice of what I was saying and were pleased to have somebody with my experience. In fact, I remember John stuck his head into the ambulance and said, 'Hi Andrew, I thought it was you!'

From there on, it was all about persevering, continuing resuscitation, going through the different algorithms and available drugs. The difference I made on the ambulance was simply being an extra pair of hands. Also, because I do this all the time, I put a very large-bore cannula that is used in cardiac surgery into a vein in Fabrice's groin that they wouldn't have otherwise been able to do. Dr Jonathan Tobin was also on board and was doing cardiac massage for a long time. When you're doing that wearing football boots in an ambulance going at high speed, you can imagine how difficult that is.

We all felt the most likely outcome was that Fabrice would die. He knows that's what we thought, and I said as much to Bolton's manager, Owen Coyle. My feeling is that he was young and very fit and had been running, so his blood circulation protected his brain.

All the doctors involved in saving Fabrice agreed that we would continue doing interviews and appearances as long as it had something to do with teaching people to do CPR and promoting public-access defibrillators.

What we often get asked is, 'What's the most important thing to stop people dying from a heart attack?' We always say that as soon as someone has a cardiac arrest, start doing CPR. You can screen the whole world but you will probably only pick up about 40 per cent to 50 per cent of those who are at risk of sudden death. Fabrice had been screened. Christian Eriksen [who survived having a heart attack while playing for Denmark in 2021] had numerous normal screenings. And Fabrice has talked a lot about this as well. A lot of lives have been saved because of what happened and applying CPR, and early defibrillation will further increase the chances of surviving. It did an awful lot of good in terms of raising the profile of the need for training in CPR and the need for more public-access defibrillators.

For a week or so, I got a glimpse into what it's like being a celebrity, and to have the press doorstepping my house, although the nature of this story meant everyone was very nice and positive.

We got invited to various ceremonies, including the BBC 999 Awards. The actress Tamsin Greig [who plays a Jewish mother in the British sitcom *Friday Night Dinner*] handed out an award. We got chatting, and she said she'd never been to a proper Friday night dinner. She came round to our house with her family a week later to experience what it's really like.

One other thing – and I think many parents can relate to this – is that when you go to pick your kids up from a birthday party on a Saturday night, by the time they become teenagers, they will say, 'Text me when you're outside'. Suddenly, after what happened with Fabrice, my kids would say, 'When you pick me up, you've got to come in and get me!'

But as extraordinary as it was that Fabrice survived, and there was no brain damage, we had another patient a few weeks later who I thought was even more remarkable. A woman came in who was 19 weeks pregnant and had had a cardiac arrest. We resuscitated her, and she came round; both mother and her baby were fine. Then, a few months later, her mother came in, having also had a cardiac arrest, and I resuscitated *her*. So, I may be one of the few cardiologists who saved lives in three generations of the same family in the same year. **"**

AND FINALLY...

Many stories of heroism emerged in the aftermath of Hurricane Katrina, which hit the southern states of the USA in 2005. One of the enduring images of the tragedy was Terrence Gray, a police officer from Gulfport, Mississippi, guiding pensioner Lovie Mae Allen and a group of kids on a rowing boat to safety. Terrence commandeered the boat to help 20 people, who were either injured, disabled, elderly or very young, to evacuate a neighbourhood where a great many homes and businesses were completely destroyed.

ALL HAIL THE KING!

———

During the week, British entrepreneur Jason Kingsley is co-owner of the successful video game and publishing company, Rebellion Developments. At weekends he gets to live out his dreams and puts on a full suit of custom-made armour, mounts his trusty white steed, Warlord, and becomes Jason Kingsley, Professional Jouster.

'Being a knight in armour forms an iconic and heroic image,' he says. 'So, I thought it would be an amazing thing to experience, and it turns out very few people knew how to do it to the standard you'd expect from a professional horseman.

'I used to ride to an Olympic show-jumping standard. My parents were of relatively modest means and sacrificed holidays to allow me to have a pony when I was an eight-year-old, which, in this country at least, is quite rare for a boy. But to have a horse that can compete at the highest level in show jumping costs hundreds of thousands of pounds.

'Now, I can afford it, but I'm not interested in that sense of competition. But my interest in history, combined with my love of riding horses, formed an obvious marriage.'

In 2015, Jason and Warlord were asked to play King Richard III and White Surrey to commemorate the Battle of Bosworth at Sudeley Castle, which was once owned by the King. 'It was pouring so we couldn't do our usual display. I thought "This is ridiculous. The King is getting wet outside!" Then I asked if it would be okay if I could ride into the castle. Because Warlord wasn't wearing shoes [and therefore wouldn't damage the castle's floor], they said "Yeah, sure". It was pretty crazy but wonderful and it had been one of my ambitions to ride a horse in a castle.

'Rebellion came about through my love of games and fantasy, but I also loved role-playing games like *Dungeons & Dragons* and *RuneQuest*, where you could escape to a different world. And you could compare what I do with riding in armour, owning horses and living on a farm as another form of escapism.'

Jason concludes, 'I think we owe it to the past to do this as properly as possible, to recapture the spirit of an age that is largely forgotten. The riding is relatively easy. All you are doing is riding in a straight line. The question is whether you've got the guts to put on the armour and do it. But I'm not particularly bothered about winning jousts, it's more about being and doing.'

STITCHED UP

———

In 2011 a book was published with a particularly eye-catching title – *A Stitch in Time: God Save the King* – **** *Hitler!*, by Anthony Casdagli, based on a period in the life of his father, Alexis.

A major in the British Army, Alexis was captured by the Nazis in June 1941 and became a prisoner of war. His diary entries from this time recorded how parcels from the Red Cross and learning how to cross-stitch helped him maintain his sanity and got him through the four-year ordeal. He also stubbornly refused to make any concessions to his captors.

His embroidery work became popular among the other officers. What the Nazis didn't know is that he was recruited as a spy for MI19 after becoming a POW, or that, even more memorably, he had woven hidden messages into a large wall hanging, which read 'God Save the King' and '**** Hitler' in Morse code.

In the same year that Anthony's book was published, a sample of his own work was displayed alongside his father's 'God Save the King' sampler as part of an exhibition at the Victoria and Albert Museum in London. In an interview with the Red Cross his daughter, also named Alexis, remarked, 'If more men embroidered, there wouldn't be so many wars'.

PEAK PRACTICE

———

Thomas Arthur Bridson was an artist who was born on the Isle of Man and returned there aged 65, having resided in various parts of the UK, including Edinburgh, Manchester and Wolverhampton. He passed away in 1966, aged 105. Thomas was the oldest person to have lived on the Isle of Man, but that isn't the reason why he is included here.

For his birthday Thomas would often climb up Snaefell, the highest point on the Isle of Man, just over 2,000 feet [600 metres] above sea level, and he continued to do this through his eighties and well into his nineties. It was said that when he reached the peak, Thomas would break into song. His obituary read, 'Artist, idealist, adventure-seeker, Thomas Arthur Bridson was a remarkable character in his day. Painting, singing, and mountain-climbing were his great interests'.

'I'M JUST TAKING THE CAR OUT FOR A FLIGHT...'

———

In 2009, entrepreneur, adventurer, derring-doer and former SAS man Neil Laughton took to the skies in the world's first road-legal flying car, on a charity mission from London to Timbuktu. Neil described his contraption as 'an ordinary road legal car, a bit like a *Mad Max*-style dune buggy. We pull out a canopy, lay out it behind the car and take off into the wind'.

The mission got off to a less than auspicious start when its designer, Gilo Cardozo, took the car out for a test drive/flight and ploughed into a small tree. Then plans to fly over the English Channel were scuppered by the Civil Aviation Authority, and he had to steer clear of the sub-Saharan region because of a civil war.

But these were trifling problems to Neil, who is used to putting his neck – and pretty much everything else – on the line. The car flew over the Strait of Gibraltar and skimmed the sand as he traversed the Sahara Desert, eventually landing at Timbuktu Airport, Mali, having hit a top speed of around 70 miles [110 kilometres] per hour, or 56 knots. Among those who saw Neil in his sort-of-magnificent flying machine, it provoked an awful lot of double takes.

AND FINALLY...

Among other feats that have raised money for various charities, Neil has led an expedition to help wheelchair-bound explorer Glenn Shaw achieve his life's ambition of seeing Mount Everest from Base Camp, jet-skied around the coast of Britain, and hosted the world's highest dinner party at over 23,000 feet [7,000 metres] above sea level in Tibet.

POLL DANCING

There are plenty of internet pranksters desperate for clicks and attention. Some of British YouTuber Niko Omilana's videos certainly fall into that category, but others are brilliant takedowns ('I Pranked America's Most Racist Man' has had over 40 million views), or mock how the modern world works, or take an issue and find an alternative way to address it.

In 2018, Niko set up the Niko Defence League, deliberately named to poke fun at the far-right English Defence League (EDL).

In 2021, Niko stood as a candidate to become London's mayor, with a campaign that was largely built on one word: 'Vibes'. Eventually, Niko set out his manifesto, which included the following five points.

1. Any McDonalds with a broken McFlurry machine will be shut down and turned into low-rent housing.
2. Boris Johnson will be forced to shush.
3. Turn off all power in London once a year and call it Londoff.
4. The price of Cadbury Freddos to go back down to 5p.
5. Free transport for under 18s and over 69-year-olds (including university students).

Setting aside the fact that every right-thinking person in London would surely support reducing the price of Freddos, Niko said his main objective was to use his platform to spread awareness among young adults to register and use their democratic right to vote. Every candidate must put down a £10,000 deposit to stand in the London mayoral election, and that deposit only gets returned if the candidate receives 5 per cent of the votes cast.

Niko received 49,628 votes, the most for any independent candidate. One could argue that when the other independents included Laurence Fox and Brian Rose – a man who once drank his own urine on TV – the opposition wasn't exactly robust.

Even so, Niko achieved what he set out to do. Yes, he failed to recoup his deposit, but given that it is estimated a YouTuber will receive thousands of pounds (or dollars) for every million views a video receives, and Niko's election video got 15 million views, then you can do the maths and work out that he also made a comfortable profit on his campaign.

The most successful YouTuber to date is American Jimmy Donaldson, aka MrBeast. He has well over 254 million subscribers to his YouTube channel and his videos regularly feature challenges that rack up crazy numbers of views. MrBeast uses a chunk of those profits to invest in philanthropic enterprises. In 2023, he paid for 1,000 cataract surgeries and 868 of those patients had their eyesight restored. He also provided the funding to build 100 wells across five countries in Africa, providing clean drinking water to around half a million people.

'DO YOU KNOW HOW TO FLY A PLANE?'

It takes around 20 hours of intense lessons to learn how to fly and land a Cessna plane. American flooring salesman Darren Harrison had to do it in a matter of minutes when his pilot, Ken Allen, suddenly fell unconscious on a flight from the Bahamas to Florida, USA, in May 2022.

The plane had gone into nosedive, dropping 3,600 feet [1,100 metres] in just 16 seconds, when Harrison, a regular flyer who would often ask his pilot questions about their work, took the controls and pulled the aircraft away from the ocean. He then grabbed a headset from the only other passenger, who was the pilot's mate, but had no practical experience in the cockpit.

Darren managed to steer the plane in the right direction but it took him a further 20 minutes to figure out how to contact anyone to explain what the hell was going on. Meanwhile, air traffic controller Robert Morgan was on his lunch break and had his feet up reading a book when a call came in from the tower that he needed to come back – and fast. Robert was also a flight instructor but had never flown this particular plane before.

He relied on an illustration on the plane's instrument panel and then began to guide Darren on his journey back to land. Robert decided Darren should land at Palm Beach International Airport, 'just so he could have a really big target to aim at'.

Video footage shows just how well Darren adapted to a life-or-death situation when landing the plane. As for the pilot, he had a tear in his aorta, was rushed to hospital and spent nine hours in surgery. His doctor later said most people wouldn't have lived long enough to make it to the ambulance. Some 16 months later Ken was given clearance to fly without the need of a co-pilot.

AND FINALLY...

The 2010 movie *Unstoppable* was inspired by the true story of how two men prevented a runaway train causing destruction in Ohio, USA. The locomotive CSX 8888, which became known as 'Crazy Eights', was pulling 47 freight cars, including two tank cars holding thousands of gallons of molten phenol, a toxic substance that is used in paints, glues and dyes. By the time the men managed to stop it all the brake shoes on Crazy Eights had been completely burned off by the heat.

'THIS IS YOUR CAPTAIN SPEAKING...'

———

Eric Moody desperately wanted to fly planes for a living. When he was initially rejected to become a trainee pilot back in 1960 on the ridiculous technicality of having a 'crooked nose', he went to see a surgeon and got it fixed. On 24 June 1982, he would have been wishing he'd left his nose alone. On that day he was the captain on BA Flight 009 from Kuala Lumpur, Malaysia, to Perth, Australia, when all four engines on the plane failed, having flown into a cloud of volcanic ash caused by the eruption of Mount Galunggung.

Eric famously announced to the 248 passengers and 15 crew members, 'Ladies and gentlemen, this is your captain speaking. We have a small problem. All four engines have stopped. We are doing our damnedest to get them going again. I trust you are not in too much distress.'

According to eyewitnesses, the passengers were remarkably calm, given that the engines were on fire.

The plane was plummeting and Eric was considering whether he would have to make an emergency landing in the Indian Ocean. Suddenly, one of the engines kicked back into life, followed by the other three, although one of them soon broke down again. Meanwhile, though, the plane was covered in volcanic ash, so touchdown was extraordinarily difficult. Yet Eric made a smooth landing to cheers and applause from all on board.

He later described the experience as 'a bit like negotiating one's way up a badger's a***'.

WHERE IS MATTHEW SMITH?

———

Behind a best-selling video game, you can usually find a small army of developers. But between 1983 and 1984 the UK charts were dominated by two games produced by one person – a 17-year-old from Merseyside who, after he 'disappeared', became a cult figure and an inspiration for a generation of gamers.

It took Matthew Smith just eight weeks to create *Manic Miner,* a platform game ranked 97th out of the 500 greatest games of all time by Polygon.

Charlie Brooker, the man behind Netflix sci-fi/horror/fantasy series *Black Mirror,* who began his career writing for *PC Zone* magazine, named it runner-up to *Pong* in his list of the five most influential video games.

Just like a band who has its first hit album, the demands of producing a follow-up took their toll. *Jet Set Willy* was an instant hit and the top game of 1984. Then nothing. Its creator's disappearance inspired the website Where is Matthew Smith? The story is comprehensively and expertly told by Matt Barton on livpost.co.uk

Matthew resurfaced in 2005 and did an interview at the Nottingham Screenplay festival. He had turned his back on video games and life at home, where he got his release from work by partying too hard, and had gone to live on a commune in Holland for five years. In his own words, 'Five years after I did it [*Manic Miner*] I was a washout; ten years after I was history...it's coming up to 20 years now and I'm a legend.'

The computer-games industry is worth billions to the UK through companies like Rockstar Games, and there are plenty of people who have had successful careers in gaming that owe a debt of thanks to Matthew Smith, wherever he is now.

As Charlie said in an interview with *Digital Spy*, 'It was a period of bedroom programming in Britain, where teenagers had been given ZX Spectrums by their parents and realised that they could write their own games.'

AND FINALLY...

On a November morning in Leksvik, Norway, in 2007, 12-year-old Hans Jørgen Olsen and his younger sister were running late for school. They decided to take a shortcut through the woods, where they were confronted by an angry moose who had been causing havoc in the village. Hans protected his sister by shouting at the moose, which caused a distraction and allowed her to run away. Then the moose attacked Hans and struck him in the back. Thankfully, his schoolbag helped to protect him. Hans was an avid *World of Warcraft* fan and remembered learning how to 'feign death' on Level 30 of the role-playing game. He lay still for 30 seconds and tricked the moose into walking away before running to school, where he was reunited with his sister.

HOPE IN THE HOUR OF CHAOS

E nrico Quarantelli was part of a group of academics from the University of Chicago, USA, sent to study the aftermath of tornadoes that had ripped through Arkansas in 1952. The expectation was that they would find panic and chaos.

The group conducted 350 interviews and what they discovered is that people had acted rationally, looked after each other, and searched for survivors. 'This is a different world than what had been assumed,' said Enrico.

In 1963 he co-founded the Disaster Research Center. He spent the rest of his life going into disaster zones, while other people were heading in the opposite direction. Even when he was old and frail, aged 76, he went to Lower Manhattan to visit the scene of what had been the Twin Towers, a few days after they had collapsed following the 9/11 terror attacks. It was said that he learned everything he needed to know simply by observing and listening.

When Enrico passed away in 2017, author Jon Mooallem wrote in the *New York Times Magazine*, 'Why do we struggle to see ourselves outside the myths Quarantelli debunked? He wondered that himself. It's hard to accept that goodness might be ordinary, hard to imagine a truth as deflating and reassuring as that.'

ACKNOWLEDGEMENTS

Dedicated to Helen & Michael

Thanks to John Andrews, Ayaz Bhuta MBE, the Honourable Artillery Company, Lysanne Currie, Dan Davies, Professor Andrew Deaner, Tara Flanagan, Tricia Garcia, Dorchester Gladiators, Behiye Hassan, Frank Hopkinson, Ian Jones, Jason Kingsley OBE, Mike Lawton, Matt Leach, Pinky Lilani CBE DL, Ruth Liptrot, Alex Mead, Geoff Meall, Kevin O'Brien, Sue Papadoulis, Andrea Price, Cris Raducanu, Mark Ranaldi, Jane Renton, Dame Stephanie Shirley, Sharon Walia, Xavier Charles Claude Wiggins BEM and Chris York.

And Miles, Leila, Mat, Yasmin & Suri.

ABOUT THE AUTHOR

———

Ryan Herman is a journalist, author and editor. He started his career on local newspapers, which provided him with his first opportunity to write about weird and wonderful news, and he has gone on to work for a broad range of publications often focusing on human interest stories.

He is also the author of two books, *Remarkable Football Grounds* and *Remarkable Rugby Grounds,* which were both shortlisted for Best Illustrated Sports Book of the Year.